Worcestershire
County Cricket Club

A Pictorial History

M. D. Vockins

Produced in association with Worcestershire C.C.C.

First United Kingdom publication 1980 from SEVERN HOUSE PUBLISHERS LTD
of 144-146 New Bond Street, London W1Y 9FD in association with
Worcestershire County Cricket Club.

Text ©Michael Vockins 1980

ISBN 0 7278 0619 X (cased)
ISBN 0 906461 05 7 (paper)

Printed in Great Britain by litho at The Anchor Press Ltd
and bound by Wm Brendon & Son Ltd, both of Tiptree, Essex

Introduction

This book has been produced for two reasons. Firstly, to aid the fund-raising programme of the Worcestershire County Cricket Club in 1980. Secondly, the Club is not well blessed with records of earlier years and whether this is as a result of the Club office moving quarters every summer and winter for many years, or as a result of the frequent floods, or even as a result of the Club assisting with the war-time paper shortage by sending unwanted paper for pulping it is difficult to tell. Whatever the reason it gives added significance to those photographs and records which have survived and which are worthy of being accessible to a wider audience and especially to an audience having a special interest in cricket and in Worcestershire County Cricket Club.

This book therefore seeks to fulfil those objectives.

It should be remembered that before the Second World War photographic techniques were not as sophisticated as those of today. As a result, action photographs, Press photographs and other similar records of the pre-war eras are much scarcer than those of more recent years. This, necessarily, has resulted in an imbalance in the photographs included in each chapter of this book.

It is not difficult, when reading this book, to believe that every player who appeared for the County was without fault. In the process of writing the book it was possible to gain the impression that it began to take the form of a collection of panegyrics. In mitigation two important factors are cited: firstly, this book is a short, historical work intended to create the atmosphere and style of each era and of the players of the time and certainly it is not a "warts-and-all" work; secondly, over four hundred players have appeared for the County since 1899 and if a number have been selected for special praise and mention here it is hoped that those players who would be considered outstanding or important in any era justly have been chosen.

If this book allows some of Worcestershire's delightfully written and photographic records to be made more widely available; if it stimulates the reader to search for himself more details in Rev. Preb. W.R. Chignell's two-volume history of the Club, in Wisden, and in the County's Year Books; if it gives a better insight into their County Cricket Club for those who are old County hands and also for those who have only recently come to the County; and if it provides for those who love the game (and particularly those who have a special interest in Worcestershire County Cricket Club) an opportunity to appreciate the endeavour, the fore-sight and ambition, the frustrations and disappointments, the fun and success which have pieced themselves together since 1865 to build the Worcestershire C.C.C. today, the objectives which stimulated the preparation of this book truly will have been achieved.

I hope you will enjoy browsing through this book and that, as you turn its pages, you will share my admiration of all those who have played a part in the life of the Club.

Michael Vockins, February 1980

To **Eileen, Helen and Morag**, and to my **Mother** and **Father**; to "**friends** in cricket" and to all who by their interest and endeavours have contributed to the life and times of the Worcestershire County Cricket Club.

Acknowledgements

This book would not have been achieved without the enthusiastic support and encouragement of **Edwin Buckhalter**, Chairman of Severn House Publishers (and a life member of W.C.C.C.), to whom I extend my warm thanks for the very pleasant and tactful way in which he has encouraged me and, most importantly, helped me avoid many pitfalls along the way.

Many friends and colleagues have taken a keen interest and have helped with suggestions or the loan of photographs or Year Books. To **Jack Roberts, Alan White, Geoffrey Lampard, Ralph Matkin, Les Jacques, Miss Hilary Edwards** and especially to **George Chesterton** and **Reverend Prebendary W.R. Chignell** goes my gratitude. I was greatly aided by being able to refer to Reverend Prebendary W.R. Chignell's two historical volumes on the Club. As these were definitive studies there was no need on my part to attempt here to produce yet another definitive work (indeed I could not hope to compete with his scholarship).

In a pictorial history the illustrations and photographs are of the greatest importance. I therefore owe much to The Editor and his staff (particularly in the Photographic Department) at Berrows Newspapers, Worcester; the Editor and the Library Staff of the Birmingham Post and Mail; the staff at the City Library, Worcester; the Press Association; Central Press Photos Ltd.; Sport and General Press Agency; Patrick Eagar; Ken Kelly; Michael Dowty and Stephen Green, Curator of the M.C.C. Museum at Lord's, for their willing and helpful assistance. To all those who have allowed me to use and to reproduce their work I owe a great debt of thanks and here warmly acknowledge their expert skills and techniques.

Tom Bader, of Tom Bader Photography, Worcester, resolved many technical problems for me and to him must go the credit for producing much of the photographic material in the form required for this publication. I welcome this opportunity to express my thanks to him.

Rob Burt, Art Director of Severn House Publishers, contributed much to the compiling of this book through his feel for the pictures and any merit the book may achieve will reflect his personal and professional contribution.

Last, and certainly not least, my wife **Eileen** typed the manuscript and produced the whole draft in a form in which the publishers could decipher even my intentions. For this, and much besides, I am grateful.

Contents

Start of the Innings – The Early Years	7
The Innings is Established 1899-1919	17
A Lean Spell 1920-1939	37
The Innings is Established 1940-1959	57
Champions At Last 1959-1979	79
Worcestershire C.C.C. – A Chronology	111
Captains Gallery	126

Start of the Innings
– The Early Years

"The Minor Counties Competition was another brilliant triumph for the Worcestershire Eleven, and all along the line. In the last issue of the Annual a suggestion was offered that Worcestershire should consider the advisability of a more pretentious programme with a view to possible promotion to the list of the first-class shires. The suggestion was carried out with fairly successful results. Against a fairly good side of Yorkshire, including more than one of the first Eleven, they made an excellent show, at least in one match, and until quite the finish looked like actually winning. Moreover they took a double first by beating the 2nd Eleven of Surrey, who had not known defeat for five years, twice. At the time this article was written there appeared to be every chance of Worcestershire's promotion to the first-class Counties for 1899."

Thus, Lillywhite's Cricketers' Annual of 1899, reviewing the previous season's cricket, heralded Worcestershire's promotion from the ranks of the Minor Counties to the realms of first-class cricket.

Berrows Journal reports the meeting held on 3rd March 1865 to form the Worcestershire County Cricket Club. This date differs from those quoted elsewhere which give the date of formation as 5th March (a Sunday) or 11th March (in which case the Journal of the same date could not carry the report of the meeting).

7

The promotion did indeed take place in 1899 "Worcestershire having at the Secretaries' meeting secured six out and home matches with leading Counties".

Worcestershire County Cricket Club had been in existence formally since March 3rd 1865 when a meeting was held at the Star Hotel, under the chairmanship of the Lord Lieutenant for the County, Lord Lyttelton, "for the promotion of the much required Worcestershire County Cricket Club".

Prior to that meeting, for some twenty years, a team representing Worcestershire had been active in the cricket field. In 1844 a Worcestershire XI lost to Shropshire in a match played at Hartlebury Common and the return match, played at Shrewsbury, also ended in defeat.

By 1847, 58 members had joined a Club representing the County of Worcestershire, and most of the games were played at Ombersley. In the following season, 1848, XXII of Worcestershire played William Clarke's All-England XI in a three-day game at Powick Ham. Clarke, John Wisden, Fuller Pilch, George Parr and their colleagues overwhelmed the Worcestershire team. A much narrower margin, but again in favour of the England XI, was the result of a similar match played three seasons later at a ground behind the Talbot Inn in the Tything. It was also in 1851 that Lord Lyttelton played for the County thereby starting the long association between the Cobham family and the Worcestershire County Cricket Club.

A further step was taken towards the formal constitution of the County Cricket Club when, in 1855, "the City" (of Worcester) and "the County" cricket clubs amalgamated. The new club was to be widely based and the ordinary man – if you like, the man in the street or the man from the factory floor – could join for an annual subscription of five shillings for which he was

> "entitled to use bats and balls and the cricket ground on three nights a week and to have the privilege of playing with the half-guinea members one night a week".

The new club played at Pitchcroft but until 1865 when the Club, now formally the Worcestershire County Cricket Club, moved to Boughton, matches were played also at St John's, and in the Arboretum at the Pleasure Gardens. Boughton was to be the Club's home ground for almost thirty years.

Worcestershire's opponents in this period were varied (as indeed

This reproduction of the painting "A Cricket Scene" by W.J. Bowden in 1852 shows a typical cricketing scene at the time of the All-England XI visit to Worcester in 1851. Note that three stumps are in use, and there appear to be no clearly marked boundaries. The fielders' head-gear would inhibit great athleticism and neither batsmen nor wicket-keeper (nor long stop) are wearing pads or gloves. The bowler is about to deliver his lobs.

were the results!) and included Warwickshire, Malvern College, Herefordshire, Cotswold Magpies, Bromsgrove School, M.C.C., Burton-on-Trent, I. Zingari, Staffordshire and Oxfordshire.

In 1895 the Club's Hon. Secretary, Paul Foley, largely was responsible for the founding of the Minor Counties Championship and in its first year of competition Worcestershire fittingly headed the Minor Counties' table albeit jointly with Durham and Norfolk. In the following three seasons, 1896, 1897 and 1898, Worcestershire reigned supreme in this competition and was thus encouraged to apply for first-class status.

Although still only a Minor County Worcestershire then employed professional cricketers as did many of the Minor and other non first-class counties. For the Club's earliest seasons in the Minor Counties competition its paid servants were Dick Burrows, Arthur Milward, Samuel Raynor (who, to quote Lillywhite's Cricketers' Annual, was a "hard working cricketer who loses his head"), Henry Rolleston, Thomas Rollings, Alexander Smith, Ted Arnold, Arnold Bird, Fred Bowley, Thomas Straw, Fred Wheldon (a footballer for Aston Villa) and Fred Willoughby (who also coached at Malvern College).

The amateurs included H.K. and R.E. Foster, G.H.T. Simpson-Hayward, G.E. Bromley-Martin and A.W. Isaac.

Another large step towards first-class status was taken when the

Paul Foley was born, on March 19th 1857, into a family of iron-masters from Stourbridge. He became associated with Worcestershire C.C.C. round about the year 1890 and was to be a dynamic and most generous Secretary to the Club. His, principally, was the idea of the Minor Counties Championship and he was the first Secretary of that competition. To bring Worcestershire up to strength for the new competition he arranged for professionals to be employed and, no doubt, contributed to their emoluments. The County's command of the Minor Counties' contests gave Foley aspirations of greater things. His promotion of Worcestershire's case, both inside and outside the County, led to the Club's admission to the first-class Championship in 1899. To complement these praiseworthy achievements Foley also took two further steps which were to have a long and profound influence on the Club. He negotiated with the Dean and Chapter to rent, for a very small sum (and an understanding that nothing unsightly would be built on the ground), the farmland beside the Severn which is now our County Ground. To transform and tend these eight acres Foley brought Fred Hunt to Worcester and so the character of Worcestershire's idyllic cricket ground and its excellent pitches was born. By the time Foley retired as Secretary and Treasurer in 1909 the County had reached runners-up place in the Championship table and Foley's foresight, ambition and leadership had been proved thoroughly justified.

present County Ground in New Road was rented from the Dean and Chapter of Worcester Cathedral in 1896. It was not, at that stage, a *cricket* ground that was rented but three fields with a hedge through the middle and a hayrick. Paul Foley encouraged Fred Hunt, Berkshire born but a Kent player, to take up the post of Head Groundsman in 1898. As in so many of the important and far-sighted decisions made at this time Paul Foley seems to have supplied the drive and inspiration and this certainly was borne out in his choice of Head Groundsman, for Fred Hunt not only turned the farmland into the cricket ground which today is so widely known and admired but he laid the foundation for the

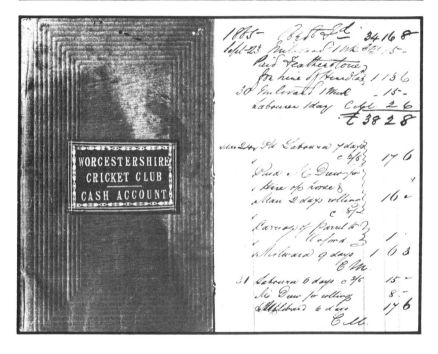

The Cash Account book of 1865 shows the expenditure for the County's first year to be £38.2s.8d (£38.14p). Such expenditure can be contrasted with that of 1929 when the figure was £6,377.5s.7d and 1979 when expenditure reached £199,802.00.

The first entries for 1866 are interesting:
"Pd Labourer 7 days @ 2/6   17/6"
"Pd Mr Drew for hire of horse and man
2 days rolling @ 8/-   16/-"

— 1897. —
BATTING AVERAGES.

	Inns.	Runs.	Most Times in an Inns.	Times not out.	Aver.
Arnold	21	697	78	2	36·13
H. K. Foster	21	705	106	0	33·12
W. H. Wilkes	8	219	56	0	27·3
E. Bromley-Martin	12	255	53	2	25·5
R. E. Foster	6	144	48	0	24
G. Bromley-Martin	16	375	114	0	23·7
Wheldon	21	433	78	2	22·17
Fereday	4	68	34	1	22·2
Burrows	18	264	32	5	20·4
Milward	20	287	59	5	19·2
Bowley	14	259	60	0	18·7
E. P. Jobson	17	279	48	0	16·7
Bird	16	174	57	3	13·5
Straw	15	81	24	6	9
G. H. Nevile	3	10	9	1	3·1

BOWLING AVERAGES.

	Overs.	Mdns.	Runs.	Wks.	Aver.
E. Bromley-Martin	189·2	59	399	39	10·9
Arnold	537·3	197	992	88	11·24
Wilson	21	5	74	6	12·2
Milward	119·2	35	260	20	13
Bird	524·3	216	884	65	13·39
Burrows	237	98	464	30	15·14
E. P. Jobson	15	3	44	1	44
G. H. Nevile	28	5	95	2	47·1
H. K. Foster	15	4	29	0	—
G. Bromley-Martin	8	2	23	0	—

— 1898. —
BATTING AVERAGES.

	Inns.	Runs.	Most Times in an Inns.	Times not out.	Aver.
R. E. Foster	19	503	147	9	29·57
W. L. Foster	13	376	73	0	28·92
H. K. Foster	23	641	75	0	27·87
G. Bromley-Martin	19	478	72	0	24·68
Wheldon	23	445	63	2	21·19
Bird	20	231	44	5	15·4
J Howard	2	30	16	0	15
Wilson	18	239	80	2	14·93
E. Bromley-Martin	21	312	50	0	14·85
E. P. Jobson	13	169	62	1	14 80
Bowley	10	134	46	0	13·4
Arnold	3	37	26	0	12·3
Milward	4	32	17	1	10·66
W. W. Lowe	2	18	15	0	9
Fereday	2	17	11	0	8·5
Burrows	19	151	54	0	7·94
Straw	19	41	13	11	5·12
A. W. Isaac	2	10	10	0	5
H. P. Keck	2	3	3	1	3
W. H. Wilkes	2	0	0	0	0

BOWLING AVERAGES.

	Overs.	Mdns.	Runs.	Wks.	Aver.
Wilson	456·3	111	1070	90	11·88
Bird	512	140	1077	81	13·3
Burrows	234·1	61	642	39	16·46
E. Martin	114·4	25	353	21	16 8
Arnold	25	9	60	2	30
Lowe	7	0	38	0	—
Powys Keck	4	1	17	0	—
Milward	7	0	41	0	—
H. K. Foster	7	1	26	0	—
G. B. Martin	2	0	8	0	—

The averages for 1897 and 1898 show the balance between the numbers of amateurs (with initials before their names) and professionals (denuded of their initials) playing in the team. The averages themselves, with the batting averages being relatively modest and the bowling averages very much better, say something about the pitches on which these matches were played, especially as the averages for 1899 proved to be more 'balanced'. Although the land at New Road was rented in 1896 Fred Hunt was not appointed Head Groundsman until 1898 and so it would seem that New Road was not used until 1899. The averages of 1897, 1898 and 1899 (the latter may be seen in Chignell's book) would seem to confirm this.

ground's characteristically excellent wickets. In so doing Hunt earned for himself a reputation for all time as one of the best groundsmen to have served the game.

By the spring of 1899, membership had increased to more than 200, and telegraph facilities for the press and seating for spectators were installed. Out and home matches had been arranged with Yorkshire, Notts, Warwickshire, Sussex, Leicestershire, Hampshire and Derbyshire despite most of those Counties requiring a guarantee of £50 (an arrangement which Sussex continued for several years!). It remained only for Paul Foley to apply the finishing touches as he did, quite literally, when, dressed in his customary brown bowler and boots, he

---

The Professionals pre 1895. This picture was discovered some years ago in the clock tower of the Pavilion. No names are given but pencilled on the reverse of the picture is "professionals 1895". Comparison with a team photograph of 1897 and reference to Lillywhite's Cricketers' Annual indicate that these players are of a slightly earlier period, perhaps 1892 or thereabouts. Whatever the date the clarity of the picture is a tribute to the photographer and the mode of dress is of interest to all, particularly when it is remembered that this was taken less than 10 years before Worcestershire became a first-class County.

13

Fred Hunt – Groundsman Supreme. Fred Hunt (seen sitting on the roller with his dog) came to Worcester in 1898, at the age of 22, from Berkshire in which county he was born near the Downs at Aldworth. Prior to joining Worcestershire he had been associated briefly with Kent.

The County Ground we know today is the result of the hard work and skill which Hunt used to transform farm land into a cricket ground. In his early seasons he was solely Head Groundsman but from 1905 until 1922 he played occasionally for the County taking 41 wickets and scoring 720 runs.

The picture reminds us that Hunt had no mechanical equipment (indeed for many years he refused the Committee's offer of a motorised roller) and his duties involved him getting up at 5.00a.m. to feed and water the horse and then set it to rolling. Neither did he have a wide range of weed-killers and his progress across the County Ground could be likened to a bird searching for worms in a lawn; every time he saw a plaintain or other weed, his pocket-knife came out of his waistcoat pocket and down he bobbed – another weed removed from his velvet turf. Thus were Worcestershire's excellent wickets prepared.

Fred Hunt remained as Head Groundsman at New Road until the end of the Second World War. Such was his standing as the leading groundsman of his time that M.C.C. called him in on at least one occasion

14

to advise on the preparation of a Test Match wicket. For many years, until the service station was built next to the Ground, Hunt farmed the land around the County Ground. In his retirement he was a familiar sight at New Road. He died in 1967. Hunt's assistant (on his right in the picture) was Reg Perk's father, later to be groundsman at the Racecourse at Hereford where Reg Parks was born.

WORCESTERSHIRE CRICKET CLUB.

WORCESTERSHIRE
v.
YORKSHIRE.
ON COUNTY GROUND, WORCESTER.
THURSDAY, FRIDAY, AND SATURDAY
MAY 4, 5, 6.

Worcestershire.	Yorkshire.
H. K. Foster	Lord Hawke
W. L. Foster	F. S. Jackson
R. E. Foster	F. Mitchell
E. G. Bromley Martin	Wainwright
G. E. Bromley Martin	Brown
Arnold	Hirst
Bird	Rhodes
Burrows	Denton
Straw	Tunnicliffe
Wheldon	Hunter
Wilson	Haigh

ADMISSION 6d.

FLYFORD FLAVEL.
PRELIMINARY ARRANGEMENTS.
FORESTERS' CLUB FETE AND SPORTS,
JUNE 5TH, 1899.
THE COMMITTEE of the above, in addition to the USUAL PROGRAMME, will add
PONY AND GALLOWAY RACES, HORSE

Berrows Journal of Saturday 29th April 1899.

15

was to be seen applying the last coat of paint to the sight-screen shortly before the Worcestershire players took the field against Yorkshire on May 4th 1899.

The County was about to open its innings in first-class cricket.

Worcestershire Cricket Club, 1899.

Date.	Club.	Against.	Where Played.	Time.
May 4, 5, 6	County	Yorkshire	Worcester	12-0
,, 11, 12	County	Nottinghamshire	Worcester	12-0
,, 13	Club and Ground	Malvern	Worcester	12-0
,, 15, 16, 17	County	Sussex	Brighton	12-0
,, 18	Club and Ground	Malvern	Malvern	12-0
,, 20	Club and Ground	Stratford-on-Avon	Worcester	12-0
,, 22, 23, 24	County	Warwickshire	Birmingham	12-0
,, 25, 26, 27	County	Oxford University	Oxford	12-0
,, 25	Club and Ground	Gloucester	Worcester	12-0
,, 27	Gentlemen of Worc.	Norton Barracks	Norton	12-0
,, 29, 30, 31	County	London County	Worcester	12-0
June 1	Club and Ground	Kings Heath	Kings Heath	12-0
,, 5, 6, 7	County	Leicestershire	Leicester	12-0
,, 8	Club and Ground	Bromsgrove School	Worcester	12-0
,, 10	Club and Ground	Cathedral School	Worcester	12-0
,, 13	Club and Ground	Malvern College	Malvern	12-0
,, 15	Club and Ground	Bournville	Bournville	12-0
,, 17	Gentlemen of Worc.	Norton Barracks	Worcester	12-0
,, 22	Club and Ground	Langley	Langley	12-0

Date.	Club.	Against.	Where Played.	Time.
June 24	Club and Ground	St. John's	Boughton	12-0
,, 26	Club and Ground	Aston Unity	Trinity Road	12-0
July 1	Club and Ground	Stourport	Worcester	12-0
,, 6	Club and Ground	Gloucester	Gloucester	12-0
,, 13	Club and Ground	Herefordshire	Worcester	12-0
,, 14	Club and Ground	Stratford-on-Avon	Stratford	12-0
,, 17, 18, 19	County	M.C.C.	Lords	12-0
,, 20	Gentlemen of Worc.	Gentlemen of War'k	Worcester	12-0
,, 24, 25, 26	County	Leicestershire	Worcester	12-0
,, 27, 28, 29	County	Hampshire	Worcester	12-0
,, 31 Aug. 1, 2	County	Derbyshire	Derby	12-0
Aug. 3, 4, 5	County	Sussex	Worcester	12-0
,, 7, 8, 9	County	Yorkshire	Sheffield	12-0
,, 7	Club and Ground	Stourbridge	Worcester	12-0
,, 8	Club and Ground	Kidderminster	Worcester	12-0
,, 10, 11, 12	County	Warwickshire	Worcester	12-0
,, 17, 18, 19	County	Derbyshire	Worcester	12-0
,, 21, 22, 23	County	London County	Crystal Palace	12-0
,, 24, 25, 26	County	Hampshire	Southampton	12-0
,, 24	Club and Ground	Herefordshire	Hereford	12-0
,, 28	Club and Ground	Boughton Park	Boughton	12-0

Members wishing to play in any Club and Ground Matches are earnestly requested to write to P. FOLEY, Prestwood, Stourbridge.

Matches were played on Monday, Tuesday, Wednesday or a Thursday, Friday, Saturday, and all started at noon.

16

The Innings is Established 1899-1919

There was to be no gentle introduction to the County Championship for the newcomers. Worcestershire's first opponents in the competition were the reigning Champions, Yorkshire, who included a youthful Wilfred Rhodes in the side which visited New Road on May 4th, 5th, 6th 1899. However, the County lost no time in justify-

The Worcestershire XI which played Yorkshire on May 4th, 5th and 6th 1899.
Back row (left to right): F. Wheldon, G.A. Wilson, P.H. Foley (Secretary), E.G. Arnold, R.D. Burrows.
Middle row: W.L. Foster, E. Bromley-Martin, H.K. Foster (Captain), R.E. Foster, G. Bromley-Martin
Front: T. Straw (w/k), A. Bird.

The team is photographed in front of the Pavilion, the completion of which Foley was most concerned about. That same building is the central structure of the present Members' Pavilion at New Road. All the players appear to be "capped" players, and grey socks and high-necked sweaters were the order of the day.

JOURNAL, SATURDAY, MAY 6, 1899.

Sport and Games.
CRICKET.
WORCESTERSHIRE v. YORKSHIRE.
A GRAND BEGINNING IN FIRST-CLASS

There was a bright genial sunshine for the opening of this cricket match on the New-road Ground. Everything was of the happiest augury for the debut of Worcestershire in first-class cricket. Mr. Foley, Mr. Isaac, and others had been at work from soon after dawn to put the finishing touches to the arrangements. Everything looked as pleasant as one could desire. As Yorkshire won the toss Tunnicliffe and Brown came out to bat exactly at noon. With the third ball of the match Wilson knocked his middle stump. 0.0.0. This was a very different from the record stand of over 500 by these two famous batsmen. Tunnicliffe luckily escaped being out of Arnold's second ball. He put a catch to W. L. Foster at second slip. The fielder was baffled by his brother, H. K., and between the two the catch was dropped. It will thus be seen that W. L. Foster was able to play. Off the next over Denton skied one, but Wheldon could not get to it. He followed this with a grand cut for four off Arnold and a three off Wilson, which went through Burrows' hands, and two singles. Denton hit another four off Arnold and then Tunnicliffe served the bowler similarly. Denton hit another four off Wilson, this third boundary inside a total of 19 and Wilson revenged himself by clean bowling his next ball. 26.2.19. Tunnicliffe swiped a ball off Arnold high into the air. Wheldon got within a couple of yards of making a catch. Mitchell cut Wilson for a four and a three and then Arnold for four, passing the fifty after 40 minutes' play. At this stage Burrows went on in the place of Arnold. Burrows' first three overs yielded only three singles. Wilson secured the next wicket. Tunnicliffe swiped wildly, intending to hit the ball into the river, but he missed it, and had his leg stump sent down. 58.3.16. The giant had batted 50 minutes for 16. Wilson's bowling was the sensation of the morning. The batsmen played hopefully, that his delivery looked simple, but the curve of the ball was too much for them. Moorhouse played on. 63.4.2. In came Wainwright, who by his sensational score last July (all will remember that 182 out of 269), snatched a victory from Worcestershire. He ran Wilson to leg for but the next ball beat him. However, it just stroked the bat, and went past the wicketkeeper for 4. Next he sent a full toss for 3. With the score 70, R. E. Foster missed Wainwright when he had made 13—a very difficult chance off Burrows. The bowlers from the New end were having bad luck. Wilson, who was bowling superbly, got the fifth consecutive wicket. Mitchell played over a very fast one, and his leg stump went. He had been in an hour for 33. Score 88.5.32. The best half of the side gone for a very moderate figure. Hirst came in and broke his duck with a lucky snick off Wilson. Wainwright sent up the 100, and off the next ball H. K. Foster missed himself. He had thus given two chances in 32. A sharp left-handed chance in the slips off Wilson. A few runs later Foster atoned for this by catching him off the same bowler. 109.6.35. Hirst, after making 9, cut one very hard off Burrows in the direction of Bird, who stopped it, but could not hold it. A few others difference would have made it a catch. He regretted it, because it only gave him a concern for his finger-ends. Arnold went on again at 116. R. E. Foster disposed of the seventh batsman by a clean catch in the slips. 120.7.14. Rhodes, the bowler, came in, and opened with a 4 of Wilson. He was the second stroke for which 4 had been run without the ball reaching the boundary, showing to those who obstinately argue the contrary that the ground is not small. Which made a single off Arnold, after, hour, and then Arnold g

SUSSEX v. WORCESTERSHIRE.
The following have been chosen to represent Sussex against Worcestershire at Brighton, on May 15 and following days:—
Sussex: W. L. Murdoch, K. S. Ranjitsinhji, C. Brann. C. B. Fry, C. L. A. Smith, with Bland, Tate, Butt, Parri, Marlow, and Killick.

M.C.C.
The Hon. A. Lyttelton, M.P., leaving the presidency of the M.C.C., nominated Lord Justice A. L. Smith as his successor—an exceedingly popular choice. Mr. Lyttelton was elected on the committee. Among the most important alterations in the that of confirming the suggested alterations by the rules of the game, these being passed as follow:—

33 (a). A batsman being out from any cause, the ball shall be "dead."
33 (b). If the ball, whether struck with the bat or not, lodges in a batsman's clothing, the ball shall become dead.
4b. They shall not order a batsman out unless appealed to by the other side.
N.B.—An appeal, "How's that?" covers all ways of being out (within the jurisdiction of the umpire appealed to), unless a batsman asking, getting out is stated by the person a-king.
2. The match (one day), unless played out, shall be decided by the first innings. Prior to the commencement of a match it may be agreed that the over consist of five or six balls.
N.B.—A tie is included in the words "played out.

The new Middlesex captain is Mr. McGregor and the vice-captain Mr. Ford.
Lord Hawke has been re-elected president of the Yorkshire club. He referred to the fact that Wainwright's benefit had resulted in £1,692. 16s 2d. being placed to his credit, and spoke in high terms of the Tinsley man's abilities and conduct. The funds of the club now amounted to £6,769. 1s 2d. A pension scheme for old players was under consideration.
Surrey won the opening first-class match, beating Leicestershire by an innings and 53 runs. Lockwood in the whole match took ten wickets for 37 runs and Brockwell scored 39. The stumps in the course of three innings were hit 23 times.
On Monday morning, the Australian cricketers opened practice at Lord's. Victor Trumper greatly pleased the critics, batting with freedom and style and plenty of power. Noble, too, showed capital form. Of the new bowlers McLeod pleased immensely. He has an easy taking style, making more of his height than do his brother, and got considerable work on the ball. Noble also bowled extremely well for a trier. Trumble, too, frequently beat the batsman.

THE LEDBURY HUNT: NEW MASTER.
Mr. Hubert M. Wilson, of the Hermitage, Holmes Chapel, Cheshire, elder brother of the Master of the Ledbury Hounds (Mr. F. T. W.) has taken over the Ledbury country.

How the local Press reported Worcestershire's first Championship game.

W.G. Grace, aged 51, leaves the field having scored an undefeated 175 for his London County XI at the end of May. The match, which was drawn, was not considered First Class. The return match at Crystal Palace was also drawn. The County Ground and the view eastward are familiar in appearance.

ing its promotion to the first-class ranks and, for two days, they completely outplayed Yorkshire. A first innings lead of 72 gave much cause for hope but fine bowling by J.T. Brown of Darfield (to distinguish him from his team mate J.T. Brown of Driffield) who took 6–19 in nine overs pulled the match out of the fire for Yorkshire to give them victory – and Worcestershire their first Championship defeat – by the very narrow margin of 11 runs.

Worcestershire had to wait until the end of the month for its first victory as a first-class County when, on May 25th, 26th, 27th, Oxford University was beaten at Oxford. Other victories in that first season were scored against Leicestershire and Derbyshire, both at home. The County Ground was "graced" during the summer by a visit from the London County team for whom W.G. Grace scored 175*.

Not surprisingly Worcestershire's players, almost at every turn were establishing records *for the County* and in the match played against Hampshire, at Worcester, at the end of July a record for first-class cricket was set up which was to remain unequalled for almost 75 years. W.L. and R.E. Foster each scored centuries in both innings of the match, W.L's scores being 140 and 172* and R.E's 134 and 101*. This was the only occasion on which brothers had performed this feat until the brothers Chappell, Ian and Greg, made similar scores for Australia against New Zealand in 1973–74. Incredibly, R.E. was to repeat the feat on two further occasions and a younger member of the Foster brethren, M.K., was to score a century in each innings, also against Hampshire, several seasons later.

This period was the era of the Fosters and whether or not it is true that Worcestershire was called "Fostershire" at the time there is ample justification for the title. All seven Foster brothers, H.K., W.L.,

Reginald and Wilfred Foster pictured after their record innings against Hampshire in 1899.

Rev. H. Foster with his seven sons, all of whom played for the County, outside their house at Malvern College.

R.E., G.N., N.J.A., M.K. and B.S., played for the County during the period from 1892 until 1934 and three of them (H.K., R.E. and M.K.) led the County for almost twenty years. They were the sons of a Malvern College House Master and sometime member of the County committee, Rev. H. Foster and his wife who, it is reputed, bowled to her young sons in the garden until they were handed over to their father for more serious training.

Perhaps the most influential of the brothers as far as Worcestershire cricket is concerned was H.K., the oldest of the brothers. He played for the County from 1892 and was Captain when first-class status was attained. A much respected captain, and universally admired, his leader-

H.K. Foster. Henry Foster's influence on Worcestershire cricket was immense and, conceivably, may never be equalled. Through his close association with Paul Foley he played a part (although he would admit Foley's to have been the greater part) in establishing the Minor Counties competition, in which he led Worcestershire to four Championship titles. H.K. was 25 years old when, under his captaincy, the County was admitted to the first-class County Championship. Apart from 1900, when his brother Tip captained the team, and 1911 and 1912 when George Simpson-Hayward filled that role, he skippered the County from the turn of the century until the end of the 1913 season, a spell of twelve seasons which no subsequent Captain of the County has yet bettered.

As Captain, Foster was a resolute, cheerfully capable and natural leader on whom the cares and responsibilities of captaincy rested easily.

As a batsman he was a tall, upright player blessed with a marvellous eye, infallible timing and the speed and coordination of a good rackets player. Although his defence was sound H.K. Foster's batting is best remembered for its consistent brilliance and the power and the glory of his off-driving. The flashing drive played between cover point and extra cover with the ball hit on "the up" comes to mind when Foster's batsmanship is recalled; he was truly a batsman of the

Golden Age. Outside cricket H.K. Foster is also remembered as one of the world's greatest rackets players. He became Paul Foley's Land Agent at Stoke Edith, Herefordshire, when he retired from first-class cricket.

Reginald Erskine ('Tip') Foster, the third of the brethren, and the only one to play for England, was the most talented of the brothers. This premise is borne out by his batting average for first-class cricket and by the records he achieved. R.E. was a slimly built, clean limbed man, blessed with a good eye. He was a consistently brilliant batsman, whose free stroke play was both elegant and crisply powerful. His off-driving and cutting were seen to advantage on fast wickets when he played with almost contemptuous ease. He was also a good fielder at slip where, it was said "he is very active and smart and a sure catch with one hand". R.E. captained Oxford University in 1900, the same season in which he was elected County Captain. He was also an England soccer international.

G.A. Wilson. Wilson was 22 when Worcestershire entered First Class Cricket (indeed the team of 1899 was a young eleven). He was a bowler of some pace even though he bowled off a short run of just a few paces. His was a round-arm style with his right arm swinging through barely above shoulder height with a slinging action. Wilson was able to bowl to a good length and gained movement off the pitch; contemporary reports suggested that he was quicker through the air than was apparent from the ring-side. It was also said that he had the power to make the ball "swerve or curl in the air – a yard, his admirers aver". Worcestershire's first opening bowler took 100 wickets for the County in 1900 and in a career spanning eight seasons he took 718 wickets in all for the Club.

ship and guiding influence during the early, formative years were of the greatest importance and value to the Club. R.E. was undoubtedly the most talented of the brethren, and M.K's batting and captaincy during the lean periods in the Twenties did much to make that period brighter, and the morale higher, than it might otherwise have been.

The Foster influence was immense both as regards the standard and the style of play. So great was their influence that for a Worcestershire team to take the field during this time without a Foster in the side was worthy of note. The Foster influence was a Malvern influence, for the College had (and happily still has) a long cricket tradition and a reputation for skill and sportsmanship in this and other sports, notably rackets. The hallmark of the best Malvern batsmen is free flowing stroke play enhanced by the wristy power of the good rackets player. This the Fosters brought to Worcestershire's cricket so that the County gained a deserved reputation for being an attractive team to watch, a sporting team to play against, and a popular team to follow. That early reputation has survived, for which much credit must go to the Fosters and their colleagues of those early seasons for so firmly establishing the standards which their successors have keenly upheld, to the great advantage of the Club.

There were of course other stalwarts in this era, all of whom gave of themselves to ensure the Club's continuing presence and its future as a first-class county. In an era when it was not customary for fielders (or the bowler!) to polish the ball nor was any pretence made to save a bowler's energies by ensuring that the ball was returned directly to his hand, G.A. Wilson, the burly right-handed round-arm bowler of considerable pace and E.G. Arnold, a medium pace bowler with a smoothly-oiled bowling action and a delivery full of guile, provided the

E.G. Arnold. Ted Arnold had been associated with Worcestershire in its Minor County days and was to become one of the best, perhaps *the* best, of the County's all-rounders. A tall, lithe cricketer with a long reach, he had the advantages of a good eye and excellent timing. As a batsman he was an upstanding player who made good use of his height, and was a good straight driver. An easy bowling action at medium-pace was coupled with his willingness to vary pace and flight in order to gain wickets. For Worcestershire Ted Arnold scored almost 15,000 runs and took nearly 1000 wickets, and in the process achieved the double on four occasions.

His prowess earned him ten caps for England and a place on the M.C.C. Tour to Australia in 1903-04. At Test level he was more successful as a bowler than as a batsman.

Note the slatted pads offering little protection above knee level and the early 'sausage' type batting gloves.

opening attack. Wilson, in 1900, became the first Worcestershire player to take 100 wickets for the County in a season. Arnold was as successful with the bat as with the ball and in 1902 he became the first Worcestershire player to complete the double of 1000 runs and 100 wickets in a season, a feat which he repeated in the three succeeding seasons. Until C.F. Walters gained his eleventh Test cap in 1934, Arnold was the most capped Worcestershire player having played in 10 Test Matches for his country and toured Australia in 1903–04 (when R.E. Foster also was a member of the Touring team).

W.B. Burns was another of Worcestershire's earliest pace bowlers. According to Sir Pelham Warner, Burns, for a few overs, was the fastest bowler he had ever seen, and he could score runs as well.

A noble servant of the County at this time was R.D. Burrows. Photographs show him as having a most unlikely build for a fast bowler, but that he most certainly was. If pace he had in plenty, accuracy was not a strong feature of his bowling. It was that lack of accuracy which accounted for the irregularity of his earlier appearances for the County. He was, perhaps, one of the earliest "good county cricketers", that noble breed of largely unsung heroes whose loyalty, dependability and honest toil has contributed so much to the game of cricket. Towards the latter part of his career greater experience and maturity brought better control and, thereby, gained him a more regular place in the

W.B. Burns. Williams Burns joined Worcestershire in 1903 at the age of 20 and played for the County until the First World War, during which he was killed. His genuinely fast right-arm bowling captured 187 wickets at an average of 30. His batting and fielding were equally energetic and capable, indeed he warranted selection as a genuine all-rounder.

In this picture Burns is shown wearing one batting glove only; this is seen so frequently in pictures of the time to suggest that the wearing of one glove may have been a common practice.

R.D. Burrows. Robert Dixon ('Dick') Burrows, at 27, was the second most senior member of that first County XI which played in the Championship in 1899, but he was to remain a stalwart of the team for nearly twenty years. Six foot tall and amply proportioned, Burrows must have been an awesome sight as a fast bowler. His 'bag' for Worcestershire was 894 wickets, at an average cost of 26.4 runs each. From contemporary reports it is apparent that when Burrows was good he was very good but when his bowling was bad it was horrid. His erratic performance and inconsistency led to his being left out of the side on occasions but when in form he was a genuine fast bowler. At a time when the pace of bowlers was gauged by the distance travelled by a bail, Burrows established the record in 1901 and ten years later he broke his own record by sending a bail a distance of 67 yards and 6 inches from where the wicket was pitched. (The thought of officials rushing to measure the distance travelled by a bail at the fall of a wicket is not without humour). Burrows gained the reputation of being a genuine, honest and warm-hearted professional. Everything conveyed by his picture and by reports of the time indicate that the reputation was entirely deserved.

The heavy buckskin boots of the day and the bandeau worn to keep up the trousers can be clearly seen in this picture.

team. Even having established that status who but a player of Burrows' ilk would have offered to appear for the County without pay – as Dick Burrows offered for the 1915 season when the County's finances were in such a parlous state. The Great War prevented the County taking up this offer.

Slow bowling was provided by G.H.T. Simpson-Hayward, an amateur (even with seven or eight professionals on the staff the Worcestershire XI frequently included more amateurs than professionals) and the last of the slow lob (under-arm) bowlers to play for Worcestershire and also for England.

Fred Bowley was the Kenyon of this Golden Age, and today his score of 276, made against Hampshire at Dudley in 1914, remains the highest individual score made for the County. The bat with which he scored those runs was presented to the Club in recent seasons by his daughter

G.H.T. Simpson-Hayward. George Simpson-Hayward was the leading spin-bowler of the County's early years. He came from Stow on the Wold, Glos., but was educated at Malvern and thus became qualified for the County. He was a right arm slow lob bowler but it must have taken considerable courage to retain and to bowl regularly a style that had been superceded by the round-arm or over-arm bowling introduced some 50 years earlier. However Simpson-Hayward gained wickets regularly and inexpensively and what better justification could he require for his anachronistic methods? Not only was his bowling fruitful at County level but it also brought its due rewards in Test Matches for England. He spun the ball like a top and was particularly successful on the matting in S. Africa where, in his first Test, he took 6 – 45.

F.L. Bowley. It was once said of Fred Bowley that when the Cathedral bells rang out across the County Ground at three o'clock they did not signify for him that there were three more hours to go until close but rather that there were but three hours left to enjoy. He was popular amongst Worcestershire's members and supporters. Bowley joined Worcestershire in 1899 and scored his first century in the following season – and he was still scoring centuries twenty-two summers later. A sound and consistent right hand bat with a powerful drive he was to be Worcestershire's heaviest and most prolific run-scorer until Don Kenyon exceeded his aggregate in the early 1950s. Tall and with a head of thick dark hair – and a magnificent moustache – Bowley was typically Edwardian in appearance. He came from Brecon and after his career of devoted service to the County ended, he coached Glamorgan C.C.C. for a spell. (They had joined the county Championship the season before Bowley's final summer with Worcestershire).

In this portrait Bowley is wearing fully-enclosed pads which barely cover the knee. A wide bandeau supports his trousers. The 'sausage' type gloves are open-palmed.

and it is displayed in the Pavilion at New Road, together with a charming photograph of Bowley.

Another highly regarded player of this period was F.A. Pearson (Frederick Albert, but known to all as Dick), a stylish and consistent

F.A. Pearson. Dick Pearson came to the County at the age of 20 and was a most consistent and popular professional until his retirement just over a quarter of a century later. In twenty-two seasons (he had lost four years to the '14 – '18 War) he scored nearly 18,750 runs and took 853 wickets. In 1923 (by then aged 43) Pearson achieved the double to set the seal on an honest and unstinting career.

Fred Root, a most lucid cricketer-author, referred to Dick Pearson as his hero. Certainly Pearson was most popular with spectators and players alike. He was completely selfless and unselfish, hated averages, and was always willing to do just what the team required of him whether it was batting up the order, down the order, opening the bowling, or taking the ball when the shine had gone from it. Whilst he was consistently successful throughout his career it was in the later seasons when the County was at its weakest that his contribution was most important. His zeal and enthusiasm did much to help the County through those difficult years.

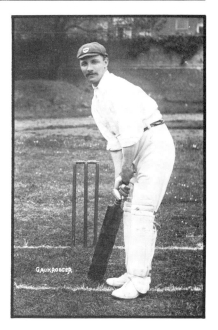

T. Straw, G. Gaukrodger and E.V. Bale. Nottinghamshire-born Tom Straw joined the County before 1899 and was one of Paul Foley's earliest signings. His wicket-keeping was well-regarded and as a batsman he was very dogged. Straw had the unique distinction of being twice dismissed "obstructing the field". He retired in 1907 although he played only occasionally after 1902 owing to a hand injury.

George Gaukrodger, born in Belfast in 1877, joined Worcestershire in 1900. Wisden says he "kept in an admirable style" and elsewhere his performance behind the stumps is reported as being brilliant. Certainly he appears to have been the best wicket-keeper of his day and was particularly helpful to Simpson-Hayward for whom he made some very quick stumpings. His batting also was useful. Ernest Bale's record of 341 dismissals stood until Hugo Yarnold passed that total after the Second World War. Bale had come to Worcestershire from Surrey in 1908 and he was a most accomplished 'keeper. Had it not been that he was a contemporary of Strudwick and 'Tiger' Smith, Bale almost certainly would have represented his country.

31

batsman and medium pace bowler who, in most seasons from 1900 until 1926 showed good form with bat or ball – and often with both!

Three wicket-keepers in turn stood behind the stumps for the County from the beginning of the century until the Great War. They were the

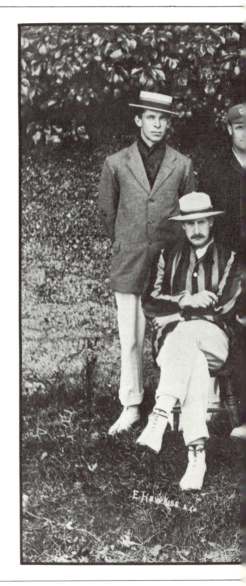

Worcestershire XI 1907. Runners-up in the County Championship, and the most successful of Worcestershire's teams until Don Kenyon's Eleven of 1964.
Back Row: J.A. Cuffe, F.A. Pearson, R.D. Burrows, F.L. Bowley, G. Gaukrodger.
Seated: R.E. Foster, G.H. Simpson-Hayward, H.K. Foster (Captain), W.B. Burns, G.N. Foster, E.G. Arnold, A. Bird.

Cuffe was an Australian whose slow-left arm bowling (100 wickets at 18.91 runs each) played an important part in the County's meteoric rise in 1907. He was a useful all-rounder who, in his ten seasons with the Club, scored 1000 runs in a season on three occasions, took 100 or more wickets in two summers, and in other seasons only just failed to reach one or other of those landmarks. Albert Bird the off-spinner was in his fortieth year in this summer of success. In ten seasons with the County his tally of wickets reached almost 300.

G.N. Foster played in half the Championship matches and headed the batting averages with 45.61. He was followed by his brothers R.E. and H.K. who also averaged more than 40 and the three of them recorded a feat which has not been equalled since the days of W.G., E.M. and G.F. Grace.

splendidly named trio of T. Straw, G. Gaukrodger and E. Bale. One imagines that in an era when 'keepers such as these would have to keep wicket to such contrasting styles as under-arm, slow lob bowling and right, round-arm, fast and furious on wickets that were not as

manicured as those of today, they must have been men of character and resilience, especially when one considers the limited protection available for their hands (had the use of beefsteak for "inners" become fashionable by then – if indeed it ever did?)

Towards the end of these first two decades as a first-class County there came into the Worcestershire team a bright star in the shape of F. Chester. For three seasons, before the Great War demanded the attention of men's minds and bodies in a deadlier contest, Frank Chester's precocious talents blossomed forth. In 1913 at the age of 17 years and 5 months he scored the first of his four centuries, and thus established a record as being Worcestershire's youngest century-maker. That record still stands today although D.N. Patel came close to breaking it in 1976. In his earliest seasons Chester showed genuine promise as an all-rounder although his medium-pace bowling was soon to give way to his run-scoring.

At the end of its first season in the County Championship Worcestershire had finished in twelfth place (above Somerset, Leicestershire and Derbyshire). By 1907, with H.K. Foster as Captain again, the County leapt to second place, but for much of the two decades from 1899 the County hovered around the position it had achieved in its first season.

On the field Worcestershire was making progress. Off the field the County's finances were a cause for concern. Income, from subscriptions and gate monies, was insufficient to keep the Club solvent and there can be little doubt that Paul Foley personally under-wrote the Club's deficits during his years in office. Later the burden was carried by other Club officers and members, Lord Cobham, Lord Dudley and Lord Plymouth with others giving a noble lead. As vital and as generous as this method of keeping the Club afloat may have been it did not provide a permanent or ideal answer. The magnitude of the problem came fully to light in 1913 when the Secretary, Mr How, suffered a breakdown in health. Those delegated to resolve the administrative difficulties discovered that the accumulated deficits totalled over £4,000. The Club had made a loss every year since 1899.

This was a serious problem indeed, and so serious was it that there were moves in the *middle* of the 1913 season to wind-up the Club. An appeal by Lord Cobham and Judge Amphlett, which gained valuable support from the local paper's "Shilling Fund", averted that final step and Worcestershire County Cricket Club survived. Despite this determined action it was not until the 1934 season that a profit was first recorded by the County.

However by 1914, fifteen years after its entry into first-class cricket,

County Cricket Crisis.
Worcestershire's Financial Vicissitudes.

As long back as one can remember, the Worcestershire Cricket Club has been in financial difficulties. They were not so acute in the early nineties as now, nor were they so acute during the days of the Minor Counties' Championship, 1895-6-7-8. Yet in those later years, notwithstanding that the team were beating everybody, public interest was relatively small, the highest total membership (in 1898) being only 333, and there was a chronic cry of lack of support. Since 1899, when the County found themselves in the first-class cricket championship, there has never been a season without a deficit on the actual working. These deficits have ranged from £140 in 1907 to £1,050 in 1909.

The present crisis is the third of its kind, and, perhaps, it is the most acute, because it comes in spite of the most urgent appeals to the public for increased patronage. The circumstances in which the Committee are about to discuss whether or not first class cricket shall be continued in Worcester, leads one to think that a record of the financial experiences of the County in first-class cricket will be interesting, and, perhaps, helpful in discussion. Below we give the membership for each year in first-class cricket, and the deficit.

YEAR.	MEMBERSHIP.	DEFICIT.
1899	798	£785
1900	1106	£155
1901	1134	£561
1902	1153	£787
1903	1292	£507
1904	1378	£400
1905	1480	£576
1906	1178	£407
1907	1054	£101
1908	1294	£140
1909	1359	£360
1910	1362	£179
1911	1354	£823
1912	1266	£547

First Crisis.

In the first seasons, when visits were paid by Ranjitsinhji, C. B. Fry, W. G. Quaife, G. Grace, and other notabilities, the gate yielded £99 per match. But even that was not enough for the existing membership, and at the end of the pavilion season, including the cost of equipping the ground, there had accumulated a total debt of £1,585. In 1900, cricket not such a novelty, the weather was fine as in 1899, and a bigger programme too much for Worcester, with the rate of raising...
fell to £49 per match.

Second Crisis.

The second crisis was more serious than the first. An unliquidated debt of £2,264 in 1903 was increased by 1907 to an amount variously stated at from £4,250 to £4,500. In 1907 there had been an increase of £120 in gate money, but there had been a reduction of working expenses, and there had been a recorded deficit of £302. About the liability to meet that £4,000 odd there arose what Lord Cobham called an "intricate and delicate situation," and it was found that extinction of the Club's debt was not to be completed by the signing of a personal cheque by Mr. Foley. Lord Cobham himself, Lord Plymouth, Sir Charles Holcroft, Mr. G. Holcroft, and Mr. Rowland Hill contributed £3,816 8s. 6d. between them. Mr. Foley gave £165 a year for three years. A little later a bazaar yielded £1,018, and other people gave £500, and these, with substantial calls upon guarantors, made an aggregate of £6,600 raised by extraordinary means to wipe out the £4,000 and the deficits on the later seasons of 1908 and 1909. In the latter year there had been two additional matches, the receipts from one of which had been allotted to Bowley, and there had been fewer amateurs and more professionals, resulting in £200 increased expenditure. A deficit of £360 had to be recorded. But during the period which led up to this crisis there had not been in practice that scheme of playing by more amateurs which had been announced in 1909 as being on foot. The annual promise of more gentlemen had not been fulfilled; but, on the other hand, the guarantee system which had been suggested then, was now found a great means of continuing the enterprise.

Third Crisis.

Exactly how much the guarantors were called upon to pay during this period was never publicly stated (except in 1909, when the figure of £600 transpired); nor were the names of the generous supporters of the game divulged. But the amount was substantial each year, and it has been considerable in the past three seasons... the season of 1910 free from... when so for nearly...

Berrows Journal reports the Club's financial crisis and the County Committee's intention to determine whether or not first-class cricket should be continued in Worcester. Whilst couched in guarded and respectful terms the implication can be drawn that Paul Foley personally had reduced earlier deficits but was, by 1907, feeling that the load might more judiciously be spread. His practical support was to continue but only the vital contributions of the County's gentry kept the County afloat until 1913 when the financial problems – and the question of the Club's continuation – again had to be faced and resolved. Article 28 June 1913.

35

Worcestershire had become established among its more senior and celebrated counterparts. The County had shown it could produce batsmen of the highest class, bowlers of consistency and endeavour, and wicket-keepers both capable and resilient. It had shown also that it could produce young players of great skill such as Chester of whom Wisden said "Probably no cricketer of eighteen had shown such promise since the days of W.G. Grace." Here was hope for the future.

That future – in cricketing terms – was to be postponed. The declaration of war in 1914 was to bring to a close the era of the Fosters; it heralded four dark years for the world, and it heralded a dark period for Worcestershire cricket after war had ceased.

Berrows Journal set up a Shilling Fund which, with Judge Amphlett's Appeal, was expected finally to put the Club's finances and its very existence on a much sounder footing.

A Lean Spell
1920 – 1939

As in many other fields the War wrought a great many changes for Worcestershire cricket. The golden era of the Fosters virtually had come to an end and the County's "honeymoon" as one of the first-class counties was over.

Now came a period of re-entrenchment, a period of frustrations, disappointments and penury when only the strength of character of the Club's officers and committee, and the loyalty of its players, members and supporters ensured that Worcestershire continued in the highest realms of the sport.

County cricket had resumed in 1919 but Worcestershire considered itself so ill-equipped that it did not re-enter the fray until 1920. Judging by the sentiments expressed in Wisden even that may have been a mistake, for in its review of the County's season the cricket bible says:

"Sorry as one may feel for Worcestershire, there is no getting away from the fact that their return to the Championship was a complete failure."

Even if those sentiments were not entirely shared in the county of the Black Pears it is not difficult to seek reasons for this sorry state of affairs. The War had ended any hopes of Frank Chester fulfilling his undoubted potential, for he had lost an arm during the hostilities. Worcestershire lost a rare gem of a player but that jewel was retained in cricket's crown as Chester joined the ranks of the first-class umpires and was to elevate that profession to hitherto unrivalled heights. Burns had lost his life in the War. Of the Fosters, R.E. was dead, W.L. had finished playing, H.K. was now aged 46 but was yet to make one or two appearances, G.N. had moved to Kent, and B.S. and N.J.A. had never played much. The one link with the great era of "Fostershire" was M.K. whose contribution to the County in the darker days after the War was as valuable as that of his brothers in earlier seasons.

Of that grand bunch of the early professionals the careers of Dick Burrows and Ted Arnold had ended by the start of the War but Fred Bowley and the faithful Dick Pearson were still in willing harness.

If Wisden thought little of the 1920 season there was precious little encouragement for its view to be altered greatly in the next ten

F. Chester. When Worcestershire sought to resume its cricket programme after the 1914 – 18 War it was without W.B. Burns, A.W. Isaac, H.G. Bache and C.G.A. Collier, all of whom had been killed in action, and R.E. Foster who had died in 1914. It was also without the County's most promising youngster, Frank Chester, who tragically had lost his right arm during the War. His unquenchable spirit and his love of cricket turned Chester's thought to umpiring and he became one of the greatest practitioners in that branch of the game. He umpired in Test Matches and was a County umpire until ill health caused his retirement at the end of the 1955 season. Within two years he had died.

Worcestershire XI 1921.
Back Row: F. Hunt (Head Groundsman), Maj. C.V. Beresford (Secretary), A.J. Powell, C.V. Tarbox, A.M. Carr, H.O. Hopkins, J.F. Toppin.
Seated: H.L. Higgins, Col. W.H. Taylor, F. Pearson, Maj. M.F.S. Jewell (Captain), F.L. Bowley, H.A. Gilbert, M.K. Foster, C.A. Preece.

The team was typical of the era with only three professionals and the side being completed with amateurs. Roly Jenkins recalls Col. W.H. Taylor recounting one occasion when he was skippering the County and his senior professional had to introduce him to seven of the team! Without the keen and devoted support of those amateurs however Worcestershire C.C.C. would have ceased to exist, and there can be no doubt that their cricket was enjoyed and was fun and that it gave another dimension to the game.

It is interesting to compare the appearance of the Pavilion (seen in background) in 1921 with its appearance in 1899, 1964 and 1974. Major Jewell's pads offer more protection, especially above the knees, than those of earlier years. There are changes too in the styles of cricket caps.

seasons, during which Worcestershire never reached higher than fourteenth in the Championship table and in 1922 and from 1926 to 1929 the County was at the very foot of the County table.

A major reason for this may well have been the unsettled nature of the team. From 1919 until 1939 there were nine changes of captaincy. Between 1921 and 1928 there was only one season when the County used fewer than *thirty* players; indeed in 1922 37 players were called on. It was during this time that Worcestershire's oldest debutant made his first – and only – appearance for the County when, in 1925, Rev. R.H. Moss, formerly of Oxford University, Lancashire and Bedfordshire, was called to the County's colours at the age of 57!

There were, of course, better players in the County XIs in this period between the Wars. Two bowlers and two batsmen stand out from among the others (indeed they would stand out in any era) for they were to produce – and to produce consistently – many magnificent performances. The bowlers were Fred Root, rejected by Derbyshire and Leicestershire, and Reg Perks, very much the local youngster who was to become a cricketing hero. The batsmen were H.H.I. Gibbons, known with the cricket world as "Doc", and his opening partner for several prolific seasons, C.F. Walters.

Root made his debut in 1923 and was to become one of Worcestershire's most successful bowlers ever. Although a most generous and

C.F. Root. Born in Leicestershire of Derbyshire parents, Fred Root was qualified and played briefly for both Counties. He later joined Dudley C.C. in the Birmingham League, in the process becoming qualified for Worcestershire.

From the moment he joined the County he did not look back. In twelve seasons he took 1387 wickets for Worcestershire at just over 20 runs apiece, and became one of the County's most successful bowlers ever and certainly the most successful bowler up to that time.

Root had previously started developing his novel "leg-theory" (in-swing) bowling. When he came to Worcestershire his theory was not well advanced as is evidenced by his total of 49 wickets in 1921 and 1922. He polished his ideas and perfected them to such a degree that in the following summer he took 165 wickets for the County. His control was such that he could control the degree of swing and cut imparted to each ball, using the old ball as well as a new one. For much of his career Root bowled without a regular partner at the other end and certainly without the close-catchers who would have made his bowling even more successful. He bowled all day and everyday, his somewhat ungainly high-stepping run to the wicket with its characteristic 'kick start' producing such rich rewards.

Fred Root, remarkably, played only three times for England. He was one of the first professionals to be granted Hon. Membership of the Club by the Committee, and seldom can an award have been more richly deserved.

R.T.D. Perks. The story of how Reg Perks came to join Worcestershire is told elsewhere in this chapter. He was required to establish a Worcestershire residential qualification for two years – during which he played for Monmouthshire! His moment came, in May 1930, for his first County match for Worcestershire, against Surrey. The County was bowled out for 40 but Reg Perks delighted in his first Championship wicket, Sir Jack Hobbs. Perks was awarded his County cap at the end of that season which marked the start of the career of a man who was to be, for 25 years, one of the most consistently hostile bowlers in County cricket.

warm-hearted man he gave little away on the field of play. He is generally regarded as having introduced to County cricket "leg theory" bowling (others later developed the theory into the "body-line" tactics used against Australia in 1932–33). Fred Root was the first (and only) Worcestershire bowler to take 200 wickets in a season, a landmark he achieved in 1925. In nine of the seasons until his retirement in 1932 he took 100, or more, wickets, a feat which his successor,

41

Reg Perks, was to perform on *sixteen* occasions. Perks came to the County's notice by making up the XI for the Gentlemen of Worcestershire who had arrived, one man short, for a game against the Herefordshire Gentlemen at Hereford Racecourse where his father was Head Groundsman. Perks was fifteen and still at school. Seldom can a day's truancy have proved so profitable, not only for the truant himself who was to become, arguably, Worcestershire's greatest – and certainly its most successful – bowler, or for those who condoned the truancy (Worcestershire Gentlemen and members of the W.C.C.C. Committee!). At a time when batsmen reigned supreme in the game

---

C.F. Walters and H.H.I. Gibbons. "Doc" Gibbons came to Worcester from the Lords groundstaff, and his neat attire and the black bag he carried immediately earned him the name by which he is remembered throughout County cricket. He was to play a most important part in the County's recovery. "Doc" Gibbons was one of the classical run-makers and an outstanding out fielder with a fine, fluent arm. Although not a tall man, he played almost every shot and played them with ease; he used his feet to move quickly on to the attack and was a very hard hitter of the ball. He went in anywhere from 1 to 6 in the batting order but it was as a splendid partner to Cyril Walters that he is best remembered. Until Don Kenyon came on to the scene nearly every batting record for the County was held by "Doc" Gibbons. Cyril Walters, like Reg Perks, had to spend two years qualifying for his new County. During those two seasons away from County Championship cricket his run-scoring instincts were being finely tuned.

Worcestershire's spectators who had seen "Tip" Foster in earlier years now recognised in Cyril Walters the same hallmarks of a class player. The facility with which he stroked the ball through the outfield masked the speed at which the ball travelled, a sign of immaculate timing. Cyril Walters' apparently effortless and exquisite stroke play has been compared by one authority with the elegance of a fencer. With his good looks, jet black hair neatly groomed, immaculate cream shirt and flannels, and his brilliant batting Walters was an outstanding cricketer. Sadly a breakdown in his health during the 1935 season ended his County cricket and he never again played for Worcestershire after that summer.

The cricket equipment and clothing shown in this picture are similar, at least in appearance, to present day equipment. The materials are heavier, and the 'spiked' gloves would be regarded as offering little protection by current County cricketers.

what a tragedy it was for the County that the careers of these two truly great bowlers overlapped for such a brief period.

Fate worked in a similar way for the County when the careers of two batsmen of great stature, Doc Gibbons and Cyril Walters, also overlapped for too short a time. Gibbons, relaxed and polished in style, was to achieve the batsman's goal of 1000 runs a season in twelve of his fourteen seasons for the County, and in three seasons he scored over 2000 runs. For much of his career he seemed to have to carry the Worcestershire batting on his shoulders. Walters came from Glamorgan to become County Secretary and, later, amateur Captain,

M.K. Foster. The sixth son of Rev. Henry Foster came into the Worcestershire side in 1908 at the age of 19 from the Malvern College XI, but overseas business commitments prevented him from playing regularly until 1914. After the War Maurice Foster played infrequently until, in 1923, he was asked to Captain the County. For three seasons his batting and sound captaincy helped Worcestershire weather a most stormy patch. In each of those three seasons Foster scored more than 1300 runs. In 1926 the captaincy passed to Maurice Jewell and, in his last full season, Foster again scored over 1300 runs. Hampshire were the County's last opponents that summer and with a commanding array of wristy cuts and powerful drives Foster scored a century in each innings (141 and 106) thus emulating his brothers' feat in 1899. It was a fine flourish with which to end a County career, although Maurice Foster was to appear on rare occasions until 1934.

and he joined the County in 1928 on the same day that a tall slim sixteen year old, Reg Perks, joined the Staff. His was an all too brief but brilliant career and in the six seasons in which he and Gibbons played together in the County XI their run-scoring was always attractive and almost always bountiful.

These were superb players but one of the great joys of cricket is the very fact it is a team game in which eleven players have to pool together their individual talents. Among the other talents available to the County in the early Twenties were the evergreens, Bowley and Pearson, who were joined by others of equal loyalty and earnest endeavour: Victor Fox, Leslie Wright and C.V. ("Percy") Tarbox.

Whilst it may not have been entirely true, it was said of the Worcestershire attack in the mid-Twenties that the opening bowlers were Root and Tarbox, and first change was Tarbox and Root!

The County still relied heavily on its amateur players in this period, players such as M.K. Foster, whose batting had all the hallmarks of his older brothers. Maurice Foster, after the retirements of Pearson and Bowley, was the mainstay of the Worcestershire batting until Doc Gibbons and, later, Cyril Walters took over his mantle. Among other amateurs who served the County delightfully and with enthusiasm were the wicket-keepers John MacLean and Bernard Quaife (also a useful batsman), batsmen of the calibre of J.B. ("Bunny") and H.L. ("Laddie") Higgins, and Gilbert Ashton, a gifted player and as good a cover-point as the County has ever had. H.A. Gilbert at times bowled superbly.

It was from the amateurs' ranks that the County's Captains were drawn. Major M.F.S. Jewell, his brother-in-law Lt. Col. W.H. Taylor, Maurice Foster, the wicket-keeper Cecil Brabazon Ponsonby and Hon. John Coventry all captained the County during the Twenties.

A major concern for the Club throughout this time was Finance (with members of Committee and friends of the Club again being called on to act as guarantors), but perhaps the greatest problem of all was putting a side into the field.

It is not difficult to envisage the formula facing the Club then: limited funds meant a small professional staff; as a consequence many amateurs were called upon; their limited and irregular availability, and the numbers thus required in any one season, led to every-changing teams. How could consistent results be expected in such trying circumstances? – and with poor results came limited income, and so the cycle went on. Evidence of this state of affairs can be seen from the Minute Books of the period.

At a meeting of the Committee held at the Star Hotel on 4th March 1932 the Honorary Treasurer reported

"The Bank overdraft was stated to be £834. 6s. 1d."

The Minute goes on to record that:

"After discussion it was agreed that the Pros. be invited to consent to a voluntary reduction of Wages, and that it be left till the return of the Secretary for him to approach them on the matter."

Apart from the obvious separation in the chain of command of the

G. Ashton

Gilbert Ashton, a member of another notable cricket family, came to Worcestershire in 1922 after three seasons at Cambridge where he gained his Blue and captained the side in 1921. With his two brothers he played for A.C. MacLaren's eclectic England XI which inflicted the sole defeat on the 1921 Australian tourists. Ashton's appearances for Worcestershire were necessarily limited, but his attractive right-handed batting, sparkling fielding and warm personality were welcomed whenever he was available.

J.F. MacLean
Between Bale, in 1920, and Buller, in 1935, Worcestershire relied heavily on amateur wicket-keepers. John MacLean, who played for the County from 1922–24 (and played but 2 games in his last season) was a wicket-keeper whose skills aroused universal admiration, particularly his speed of stumping which was remarkable, as 23 stumpings from 55 first-class dismissals indicate.

H.A.Gilbert

H.A. Gilbert came into the Worcestershire team in 1921 fourteen years after his successful debut season for Oxford University, during which he had taken 44 wickets at 15.52 runs apiece. "Balmy" Gilbert was to play two full seasons only for the County but manfully helped out on occasions until 1932. He was a bowler of undoubted class who, at right-arm medium-pace, used flight, variation of pace and 'cut' to gain his wickets. It was generally considered that this modest, enthusiastic cricketer would have played for England if he had been able to devote more time to the game.

B.W. Quaife

Bernard Quaife played for Warwickshire before he joined Worcestershire in 1928 as a right-handed batsman. Throughout nine seasons with the County he played many valuable innings for the side, particularly when the going was hard and rear-guard action was called for. In 1930 he gallantly made himself into a wicket-keeper and so successful was he in this that he held the position until Syd Buller became qualified. On numerous occasions, in the absence of Cyril Walters or Charles Lyttelton, this indispensable cricketer led his adopted County.

Bunny and Laddy Higgins were typical of many of the amateurs who willingly turned out for the County in the Twenties and thus kept the Worcestershire flag flying. Capable rather than gifted, sound rather than brilliant, they nevertheless performed valiantly with the bat. Their records are remarkably similar, each scoring around 3500 runs at an average of about 20. The brothers were both right-hand batsmen; J.B. occasionally bowled slow left-arm whilst his younger brother was a splendid cover

H.L. Higgins   J.B. Higgins

point. In his cricket days J.B. was employed by Cadbury's in India and played for the County in his summer leave. A disagreement between the two captains led to his umpiring the third Test between England and India, at Madras, in 1934. Laddy Higgins was an excellent rugger player, who achieved selection by the Barbarians.

47

decision-makers and the decision implementors, note that "the Pros. were asked to consent to" – not to discuss, or to consider – a "voluntary" reduction in their income!

And what was their income? A Committee meeting later that summer agreed

"That payments to professionals next season be as follows: £2 per week all the Year round. In addition £4 for each Home match, £7 for each Away match, £2 for every win."

The Club's finances did not allow such terms to be applied too widely and we read in the Minutes of that same meeting *"Mr Kempson said that he was authorised to state that Kidderminster, Dudley and Stourbridge C.Cs undertake to provide at least one amateur for each match next season."*

What did these sort of terms and the presence of a large number of amateurs mean to the County's professional cricketers? They were

Major M.F.S. Jewell. The revival – and survival – of Worcestershire County Cricket Club after the 1914–18 War owed much to the devotion and determination of Maurice Jewell and his colleagues. Jewell had appeared briefly for the County in 1913 and again in 1914 and then in 1920 he was asked to Captain the team. With less than a handful of professionals available it was a far from easy task but Jewell accepted the challenge with great zeal. He was a shrewd Captain, and a firm disciplinarian. A right-hand batsman, Jewell was sound in defence but also keenly disposed to attack. As a fielder at a time when fielding was not the athletic art it is today he was one of the sounder men. Occasionally he bowled, slow left arm. 1926 was to be his best season when he scored 1000 runs, including two centuries against Hampshire, and came second to Root in the bowling averages. His career record of 4114 runs at an average below 20 and 104 wickets, at a cost of more than 33 runs, gives a more accurate assessment of his cricketing skills. It does not convey with any accuracy the immense importance and value of Maurice Jewell's contribution to Worcestershire which truly was beyond measure.

accepted as "occupational hazards" or, perhaps more correctly, as facts of their working life. And that working life contained other drawbacks which, on occasion, had to be accepted as is apparent from the Minutes of the Selection Committee meeting held on 13th July 1934 (at which teams for matches starting on 18th July and 21st July were selected):

> "*Team chosen v. Somerset* 18/7/34. Include Mr. A.P. Singleton instead of Mr. Humphries. Mr. Quaife to Captain. Otherwise same as v. Lancs. Drop Howorth to 12th Man if Lyttleton can play."

This is quoted, not as any indication of the relative cricket merits of Dick Howorth, the professional, and the Hon. Charles Lyttleton, the amateur, but to give an insight into the cricket world of this time; its finances, how they affected the professionals, the generous support and assistance provided by an army of amateurs, and the total effect of such arrangements on the playing results of the team.

Maurice Nichol burst on to the County scene in 1928 with a century on his first-class debut, against the West Indies. He was then aged 24, and for six seasons his compact but fluent batting was to bring great pleasure to the County's supporters. He was a superb cover-driver and a master of the hook which he played with almost contemptuous ease. As is true of many great players the best bowlers drew from him some of his finest innings. Despite bouts of ill-health (in 1932 he played hardly at all) Nichol scored 17 centuries in six seasons and amassed nearly 7,500 runs. A career of great promise had ended when he was found dead in his Chelmsford hotel bedroom (an enlarged heart was the cause) on the morning of the Bank Holiday game with Essex.

It is against such a background that Maurice Jewell's role should be examined. He was a County Captain of his time. An able but not gifted performer frequently was appointed Captain of a County simply because he was an amateur and because he had qualities of leadership. Such a philosophy was applied by almost every County at this period (and for a considerable number of years on).

H.H.I. Gibbons. "Doc" Gibbons here kitted out for practice illustrates that it is not only the present generation of cricketers who save their 'whites' for match days.

Just visible in the background is a most important member of the County's staff – the horse. By 1934 the County Committee considered the time had come for a mechanised roller to be purchased. Groundsman Hunt would have none of this despite assurances from the Committee that his working day would start later (there being no horse to feed before work commenced, and rolling would be done more quickly by motor power). Even the offered £25 p.a. reduction in wages (to account for the shorter hours) would have left a small profit (for it had cost about £40 p.a. to feed the horse), but he was not to be persuaded.

At a Committee meeting in 1935 it was reported that "Our horse (34 years old) had had to be destroyed".

Hunt continued to use the horse roller, now pulled by man-power, until near the end of his career when the heavy roller was collected from Shrub Hill station – by another member of Hunt's staff.

Bowlers in command. In 1937 four of the County's bowlers each took more than 100 wickets during the season.

R.T.D. Perks	R. Howorth
141 wkts	105 wkts
Av. 21.29	Av. 29.94
P.F. Jackson	S.H. Martin
102 wkts	114 wkts
Av. 25.91	Av. 20.41

Sid Martin also scored 1000 runs in the summer and thus recorded the first of his two "doubles" for the County. The tall South African all-rounder scored over 10,000 runs with attractive stroke play and, with his right-arm medium pacers, took nearly 500 wkts in eight seasons with Worcestershire.

Major Jewell's was a firm, authoritative (and almost certainly unquestioned) leadership. If the truth was known he probably did not relish the task of captaincy but if the County felt Maurice Jewell was the man for the job then his loyalty and sense of duty ensured that he undertook that task to the very best of his ability.

J.S. Buller. After nearly fifteen seasons without a regular professional wicket-keeper the County employed a Yorkshire man, Syd Buller, as the County 'keeper. His first full season was 1937 and it was reported that "he kept wicket excellently and he is by no means negligible with the bat". Buller's was a neat and quietly efficient style of 'keeping as was to be expected of a man who was always immaculately turned out.

In 1939 he was badly injured in a car accident. Then came the Second World War and the cessation of County cricket. When cricket resumed Buller was unable to recapture his form of earlier years. He was appointed County Coach but later became a County and Test umpire; indeed one of the very best.

His enthusiasm, and his determination for the future success of the County were boundless. Jewell, aware that finance limited almost every aspect of the Club's activities, including its ability to employ more professionals, sought to remedy the situation.

Which other County Captain has formed his own Concert Party with which, with the help and encouragement of family and friends, to tour the county raising funds for the Club? Maurice Jewell did that – and much more besides. When his playing days were over he was to become in turn Chairman of the Club, a Trustee and, later, its President. Later still his eminent and unstinting service to Worcestershire was acknowledged by his election in 1956 as an Honorary Life Member of the County Cricket Club.

As the Twenties gave way to the Thirties there were hopes of better things ahead. Maurice Jewell's Concert Parties had been backed up by bazaars (grand affairs lasting two or three days), whist drives and raffles and – in every fourth year – that financial saviour of so many Counties through the years, a visit by the Australian touring team.

With the easing of the financial problems the playing strength very gradually was strengthened. George Brook, a 35 year old leg-spinner who took more than 450 wickets in six summers, came to the County from the Lancashire League. P.F. Jackson, an off-spinner who could also bowl accurately with the new ball at medium pace, had joined the staff in 1927. The following season C.F. Walters, an amateur, came from Glamorgan as Captain and Secretary. He brought with him batting skills that matched the best of the Fosters of an earlier era and were to be seen in T.W. Graveney in a future era. In 1928 Maurice Nichol (whose career ended tragically with his death at Chelmsford

---

Hon. C.J. Lyttelton. Charles Lyttelton's place in Worcestershire's cricket history rests mainly with his splendid captaincy of the team from 1936 until 1939. Undoubtedly he had a good side under him, but their respect for the Captain would not have been so high had he not been a vigorous and capable player. Lyttelton was a better cricketer than he himself believed. As a stroke player and one of the hardest hitters of the ball he sometimes allowed batting theory, which fascinated him all his life, to inhibit his natural inclination to play shots. He was a courageous close fielder and of his bowling the County Year Book said he "might with advantage bowl more frequently".

during the Essex match in 1934) made his debut for the County and gave every appearance of being an England player in the making. Here then, with the experienced Root and the youthful Perks, Gibbons and Walters also available, was the nucleus of a successful team. And yet it was not to be!

Worcestershire's players were producing good performances, but as a team their results were disappointing. This paradox cannot be better illustrated than by the 1928 season in which *five* players each scored more than 1000 runs, Fred Root did the "double" – and yet *not one* match was won by the County.

That season was Maurice Jewell's last as Captain although he was still to appear occasionally for the County. The frustrations and setbacks might have encouraged lesser men than those then associated with the County to give up but Worcestershire's followers must be ever grateful to those whose loyalty and undiminished enthusiasm kept the County flag aloft. The frustrations they faced were recalled by Jewell in his later years when, looking back to those seasons in the mid-Twenties, he remembered the County, which previously had lost something like 23 consecutive games, scoring heavily against Hampshire. With a lead of 500 runs he found himself in a position even to consider declaring, a most unusual situation for the County at that time. So unusual was it that the Senior Pro., Fred Root, had to be consulted. "I should declare, Sir" was his advice, given in the hope of getting early Hampshire wickets that evening. Three Hampshire wickets *were* taken for about 60 runs before the close, and one imagines that there must have been much tossing and turning that night in the beds of Worcestershire players dreaming of the unusual prospect of a win ahead. That bright prospect was dashed by the wide bat of Phil Mead who batted for the whole of the next day to save the game for Hampshire, who finished with a score of 424–4. Such did seem to be Worcestershire's luck – almost permanently – at the time!

In the early seasons of the Thirties Worcestershire batsmen held sway. 1933 was the season in which three batsmen, Gibbons, Walters and Nichol, all scored over 2000 runs – and yet the County was third from bottom of the County table. Another brilliant batsman, the Nawab of Pataudi, joined the side in 1932 but in seven seasons he was able to play in only thirty-seven games.

As the Thirties progressed, the team's strength swung more from batting to bowling. Root had retired, but Perks was now in full swing. Howorth was making the progress that would make him a Test class spinner and very useful all-rounder in County cricket; he was to become

C.H. Palmer. Today Charles Palmer is best known as a *force majeur* of Leicestershire C.C.C. and a recent President of M.C.C.. Worcestershire supporters of the years either side of the 1939 – 45 War fondly recall Palmer as the Bromsgrove School master who played so attractively for the County in July and August each summer until the end of the 1949 season when he joined Leicestershire as Secretary-Captain. Charles Palmer was born in 1919 at Old Hill (which the County's cricket supporters would argue falls within the Worcestershire boundaries) and was educated at Halesowen Grammar School. His bowling officially described as "right medium" often owed more to real elevation (as opposed to flight) with the ball dropping from a great height to land between batsman and stumps. An analysis of 8 for 7 against Surrey showed the effectiveness of the style.

one of the best all-rounders the Club has ever had. In 1937 he was one of the quartet of bowlers – Perks, Syd Martin and Peter Jackson were the others – who each took more than 100 wickets in the season. Syd Buller had joined the County from his native Yorkshire, and proved a more than useful wicket-keeper. Later, he was to become a Coach for the Club and, later still, a Test and County umpire of the highest class. Towards the end of this decade another wicket-keeper, Worcestershire born and bred, was to find a place in the County XI. Hugo Yarnold was to become one of the best and most successful of the County's 'keepers.

In the years before the 1939 – 45 War the County was led – and led with gusto, great determination and good humour – by Hon. Charles Lyttelton, later to become Lord Cobham. He was warmly regarded and respected by his players. If any man had the personal qualities to lead a successful team it was Charles Lyttelton. By this time Doc Gibbons, still in his bountiful prime, was being supported in scoring runs by Eddie Cooper, a Lancastrian 'import', Charlie Bull (who died tragically young in a car accident) and the abundantly talented young local cricketers Charles Palmer and A.P. Singleton. Buller and Yarnold

Worcestershire XI 1936: Standing (L to R): B.P. King, J.S. Buller, P.F. Jackson, S.H. Martin, F.B.T. Warne, R. Howorth
Middle row: H.H.I. Gibbons, B.W. Quaife, Hon. C.J. Lyttelton, R.H.C. Human, R.T.D. Perks
Front row: L. Oakley, C.H. Bull, A.P. Singleton, J. Horton, R.D.M. Evers.

shared duties behind the stumps, Perks, Howorth, Martin and Jackson were the successful bowlers (with the young leg-spinner Roly Jenkins not yet firmly established in the side), and Worcestershire rose to seventh in the County Championship that season. The dark days were over! – or were they?

Just as Worcestershire was proving it had overcome its problems of the lean years following the First World War and now had built a team with the abilities and the conviction to challenge all, the County was to be denied the opportunity to show its new found strength and confidence. The World was again at war.

56

The Innings is Established 1940 – 1959

County cricket ended with the onset of War and although some excellent and entertaining matches were played during war-time most often these were to raise funds or to provide a relief from the horrors of War.

The War ended the County careers of Doc Gibbons, Charles Lyttelton and Sid Martin, and also took huge and irreplaceable slices from the careers of fine cricketers such as Perks, Howorth, Jackson and Buller, men who would have been in their cricketing prime at the time of conflict. The younger brigade, men like Sandy Singleton, Charles Palmer and Roly Jenkins, who had just started careers so full of promise before War was declared, were able to resume their progress, but even for these men such a huge gap in their careers could hardly be retrieved. Perhaps saddest of all was the loss of Reg Perks' Test career, for he had shown himself to be a bowler of Test class and had played for England at home and abroad in the seasons immediately before September 1939. By the time hostilities had ceased he was no longer in the full flush of youth, and although he was to give truly admirable service to his County for another ten seasons his chance of Test cricket had gone.

Sandy Singleton captained the side in 1946, his only full season for the County before leaving for a new life in Rhodesia. After six summers without serious cricket the public gave a warm welcome back to the County game and to its players who undoubtedly shared the joy of commencing again a more pleasant conflict. Singleton was the man for the hour and under his leadership the team, and their supporters, enjoyed their regained freedom of spirit. To hear one senior and experienced professional talk so glowingly of Sandy Singleton's captaincy (and this from a man who played under a number of captains) provided a testimony to Singleton's role in getting Worcestershire's innings away to a good start in this new era. Singleton's team included Perks, Howorth, Jackson and Jenkins to bowl whilst runs came from Eddie Cooper, Palmer, the youngsters Don Kenyon and Martin Young (who later joined Gloucestershire), and the two former Warwickshire players R.E.S. Wyatt and A.F.T. White. Wicket-keeping was still shared by

Worcestershire XI 1949:
Standing (L to R): F. Cooper, D. Kenyon, E. Cooper, R. Howorth, R.O. Jenkins, H. Yarnold

Seated (L to R): R.T.D. Perks, R.E. Bird, A.F.T. White, R.E.S. Wyatt, P.F. Jackson.

Buller and Yarnold, and the Captain provided a splendid example at batting, bowling or fielding. A day on which his fielding lapsed from its usual infallibility was during the match against Gloucestershire at Cheltenham when Perks, with a wonderful bowling display, took 9 – 42 and would have taken all ten wickets for the only time in his career but for his Captain dropping the last man off a "simple" catch at slip.

That first post-war season of 1946 saw the County finish the summer placed in the middle of the Championship table, a position around which they were to hover for almost 20 years never quite reaching the top nor yet plumbing the table's depths.

The best season was 1949 when the County finished third, immediately behind Yorkshire and Middlesex who tied for the Championship title. Roly Jenkins took a hat-trick in *both* innings against Surrey

L. Outschoorn. Christened Ladislau, but to the cricket world he is Laddie Outschoorn. In his career with the County, which spanned the years 1946 to 1959, he scored over 15,000 runs (at an average nearing 30) and hit twenty-five centuries. In the field this slight man from Ceylon with the engaging smile was a predatory fielder. In all he took 274 catches, most of them fielding close in at slip or gully where a keen sense of anticipation ensured that few catches were missed and some remarkable ones were held.

G.H. Chesterton. George Chesterton was born in Shropshire and is an Old Malvernian and Oxford Blue. He returned to Malvern as a member of the College Staff and was thus available each year to play for the County in July and August. Each summer he went straight into the side and provided a relief force for the County's bowlers who, understandably, were sometimes feeling a little jaded by that stage in the season (the Championship programme then still comprised 32 matches). He bowled right-arm medium-pacers with great stamina and good cheer, never paling at requests for twenty and thirty overs a day. His accuracy was metronomic as 168 wickets (at 19.87 runs each) in eight part seasons indicate. The boys at Malvern could have no finer example of the bowlers' creed of length and line than that provided for them by their cricket master. In recent years he has been succeeded in that post by Alan Duff, also an Oxford Blue and Worcestershire amateur, indeed one of the last amateurs to play for the County (in 1960 and 1961).

that season and Laddie Outschoorn, a batsman who mixed the unorthodox with the orthodox, took 55 catches out of the record bag taken by the County's fielders the summer. A record achieved *against* Worcestershire in that same season was J.D. Robertson's undefeated 331 scored in the day for Middlesex, at New Road.

This was still a time of amateurs and professionals. In addition to the

A.F.T. White and D.G. Bradman. Alan White, of Uppingham. Cambridge University, Warwickshire and Worcestershire tosses up with The Don before the County's match with the Australians in 1948. It was White's second year as skipper. He was to prove a genial and popular Captain and his easy good nature rubbed off on to the team. Business interests required more of his time in 1949 and White shared the captain's responsibilities with Bob Wyatt; together they took the County to third place in the Championship. Bradman, in 1948, was making his fourth visit to Worcester. He had marked each of his previous visits with double centuries but on this occasion he "failed" and could only manage 107 in the first innings; the Australians were not required to bat a second time!

The young spectator to Bradman's right is Peter Richardson, then a 17 year old school boy, who was to play for the County the following summer.

R. Howorth. Lancastrian Dick Howorth played first for the County in 1933 but his earliest seasons gave little indication of the deeds to come. In thirteen seasons, including those less productive first seasons, he scored over 10,000 runs for Worcestershire and took well over 1200 wickets. 7–18 was his best return, against Northants. He first achieved the-double in 1939, then came six years of War, but in 1946 and 1947 he repeated that all-round feat. Only Ted Arnold of Worcestershire's players has achieved more.

1947 was his *annus mirabilis* when he scored 1500 runs and, not content with that, dismissed 150 batsmen. The late and deep flood of that year left a residue of powdery silt which may have aided those bowling figures but it could not also have accounted for the weight of his run-scoring.

Normally Howorth was not a great spinner of the ball. His was the smooth, graceful and almost languid action of the classical left-arm spinner, with great reliance placed on length, line and subtlety of flight. When batting, the same classical style was absent. There was a grimness about his defence – "they shall not pass" – but a vigorous delight when on the attack.

There was much that was enigmatic about Howorth the cricketer. The cap worn at a jaunty angle suggested a carefree approach which the skill of his bowling and the determination of his batting denied. Outwardly laconic and taciturn he possessed a wry sense of humour and a warm heart. He thought much, and deeply, about the game and its players (and he still does). Dick Howorth has always been willing to help other players and to share with them his vast store of knowledge and his thoughts on the game for which he has the greatest affection.

amateurs who returned to the fray in 1946 there came Lt. Cdr. Mike Ainsworth, a tall, hard-hitting batsman whose batting recalled the style of the amateurs of earlier eras; George Chesterton, an Oxford Blue and Old Malvernian, and a medium-fast bowler of immaculate con-

P.F. Jackson. "Some impressive off-spin bowling by Peter Jackson" was among Don Bradman's reminiscences of his visit to Worcester in 1948, but Jackson's impressive bowling was not restricted to that season (when, in fact, he was not at his very best). Between 1929 and 1950 he took over 1100 wickets for Worcestershire mostly with his off-spinners but also with medium-paced out-swingers which he bowled from time to time (and with great purpose) when the County's bowling had little depth. Fair haired, wide shouldered and with hands the size of proverbial meat plates, Jackson bowled with a tall, upright action and he could keep one end quiet all day. His pace was varied to suit the pitch but generally he bowled slightly quicker than is normally expected of an off-spinner. Certainly batsmen discovered that his pace often made it difficult to get out in time to hit him off his length or stifle the spin, and on a wicket that offered assistance he was almost unplayable. His huge hands served him well at short leg and "c.Jackson b.Root (or Perks)" appeared frequently in the score book. Few Worcestershire players batted below him in the order. A kindly and modest man he was, perhaps, too modest and sensitive about his bowling at times, for many of his colleagues believed him capable of being an England player.

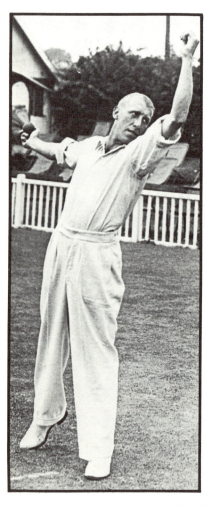

R.T.D. Perks leads the Worcestershire team on to the field. 1955. The constitution of Worcestershire's new young bowler in 1928 gave cause for concern, at least to the Club Chairman, Lord Doverdale. He decreed that young Perks should be sent, at his expense, for holidays at Weston-super-Mare and was to take egg-and-sherry each time before he went into the field. His Lordship also found winter employment, tree-felling, to strengthen Perks' physique. Those measures were a success for they carried Reg Perks through a career spanning twenty-eight years and which culminated in his appointment as the County's first professional Captain.

Following the Captain, in this picture, are Peter Richardson, George Dews, Hugo Yarnold, Bob Broadbent and Roly Jenkins. The South African tourists look out from the Visitors' dressing room, and the Club office can be seen to the right of the Pavilion.

---

trol and economy; Peter Richardson, from the Cathedral School at Hereford, was an attractive bat who later joined the ranks of the professionals and, some would say, lost the freedom in his batting. The professional staff was strengthened by the signing of players like George ("Gentleman George") Dews, a good bat, brilliant fielder and splendid team man. Bob Broadbent was another fine fielder, attacking batsman and a player who, for fifteen seasons, was to contribute at least as much to team morale by his character as his cricketing prowess.

One surprising feature of this more successful period was the frequency of changes in the captaincy. Singleton had given way, after one season, to the Cambridge Blue, Alan White, who took the helm for two cheerful seasons before sharing duties with Bob Wyatt in 1949. Wyatt, formerly of Warwickshire and England (for whom he appeared in 40 Test Matches), and now in his fifties, led the side for the next two seasons during a period of transition. By the close of Wyatt's period of captaincy Howorth, Jackson and Cooper had retired from County cricket, Palmer had joined Leicestershire as Secretary and Captain, and White and Ainsworth only rarely were available.

Dick Howorth had taken over 1200 wickets for the County with his classical left-arm spin, and in each of nine summers he took more than 100 wickets; although most often a middle-order bat he frequently opened the innings for the County. With over 1000 wickets and 10,000 runs for the County Dick Howorth deservedly stands alongside Worcestershire's other great all-rounders Ted Arnold, Martin Horton

Worcestershire XI, Scarborough 1957. Left to Right:
D.W. Richardson, R.G. Broadbent, L.J. Coldwell, G.H. Chesterton, M.J. Horton
R. Booth, J.A. Flavell, P.E. Richardson (captain), D. Kenyon, G. Dews, L. Outschoorn.

P.E. Richardson. At the Cathedral School, Hereford, Peter Richardson's cricket talents were patently obvious and he came from the School XI to play for the County as a free-scoring, left-handed batsman. He was an attractive stroke-maker but later some of the amateur's freedom went from his batting and he became more compact, less vulnerable, and a more productive opening bat. He had great success as an England opener, averaging over 37 runs per innings in a career of 34 Test Matches.

and Basil D'Oliveira. His deeds on the field of play most certainly ensure him a place in the County's Hall of Fame but the contribution made to Worcestershire by this seasoned, immensely knowledgeable and kindly cricketer did not end when he hung up his boots; he was to become a most valuable and influential member of Committee and many of the teams and players of recent seasons bear testimony to his judgement of a cricketer. Peter Jackson was another whose stalwart and loyal service to the County exceeded the many overs he bowled for Worcestershire. It must be remembered too that in his earliest seasons Jackson, whose career started before Howorth's, was playing in a team whose bowling, apart from the by-now ageing Root and the raw Perks, was unexceptional. It was by no means unusual for Peter Jackson to take the new ball and, after some opening overs at medium pace, to take a break before returning to the attack as an off-spinner, at which art he was most proficient.

The captaincy passed to Ronnie Bird in 1952 and for three seasons he proved to be a confident and purposeful skipper. Sadly his confidence was not reflected in the County's results and Worcestershire again found themselves in the lower half of the table.

For the 1955 season the County Committee appointed the Club's first professional Captain and, in Reg Perks, one of its most popular players of all time. His appointment recognised his vast experience and knowledge of the game, his long and loyal service to the County, and the very high respect in which he was held by team colleagues and opponents alike. When, at the end of that season, Perks retired he left behind a game better for the contribution he had made to his County and country since entering County cricket some 27 years earlier. In his last match for the County he completed his 100 wickets for the season, the sixteenth consecutive season in which he had performed that feat. He left the game with many happy memories, and above all he left as a much-loved and respected cricketer.

Peter Richardson, twenty years Perks' junior, was the man chosen to succeed the great fast bowler. He led a side which included Perks' bowling successor, J.A. Flavell. The County seemed blessed with bowlers of some pace at this time. K.J. Aldridge, D.B. Pearson and K. Lobban were all tried before L.J. Coldwell became Flavell's regular partner in an opening attack that became the scourge of opposing batsmen. M.J. Horton, a young, Worcester born all-rounder was establishing himself in the team as an off-spinner and prolific batsman. Roly Jenkins, that Clown Prince and enormously gifted of cricketers, was still bemusing countless batsmen (and, occasionally, members of his

R.O. Jenkins. A product of the Worcester Amateur Evening League Roly Jenkins is the "local boy who made good" – and how well did he do it! That rare being (certainly today), a leg-spinner, Roly went from amateur club cricket to play for England and, on the way, completed an immensely successful County career.

Jenkins' approach to the wicket was crab-like but decidedly purposeful. When he released the ball it spun enough to hum; no recent cricketer has spun the ball as much. There was a determined combative approach to his cricket; workman-like is too mundane a description because he was, too, an artist but it is an apt description for Jenkins certainly worked, and worked hard, at his game. By his artistry and his endeavours he took 1148 wickets for the County and he made himself into a batsman who scored over 10,000 runs in first-class cricket. He twice achieved the double and, in 1949, at Worcester, bamboozled Surrey by taking a hat-trick in each of their innings. A true character who probably talked out as many batsmen as he bowled out, but who enjoyed his cricket and, in return, gave much enjoyment.

own team) with his characteristic mixture of top-class leg-spin, anecdotes, and determined but warm-hearted aggression. The Captain was a prolific run-scorer, both for the County and for England, Don Kenyon took the attack to opposing bowlers and assumed such command over them that never for a moment were they allowed to dominate him, and Martin Horton showed himself capable of making big scores. Bob Broadbent and George Dews were at the peak of their inestimable service with the County and the Captain's younger brother, Dick, was soon to establish himself as a free run-scorer and a prince among close fielders.

Despite this multitude of talent, success apparently had made a note permanently to avoid Worcestershire. Promise there certainly seemed

R.G. Broadbent. What a great catch of Bob Broadbent's to dismiss Bill Edrich of Middlesex. The picture illustrates Broadbent's wholehearted approach to the game, and certainly the customary excellence and adroitness of his close catching is clearly demonstrated. Broadbent was a stylish, hard-hitting right-hander who scored nearly 13,000 runs for the County between 1950 and 1963, and who would have scored many more but for the nervous hesitancy which sometimes marked the start of his innings. In full flow he was a merciless marauder of bowling. His bag of 298 catches for the County has been exceeded only by Dick Richardson, Dews, Headley and Kenyon. A true County stalwart.

---

to be, even occasionally a near miss, but success itself seemed impossible to capture.

    Off the field the County was having greater success. Brigadier Mike Green had been appointed Secretary of the Club after the War and he brought as much drive and foresight as had his predecessor, Paul Foley, many years earlier. He is not given formal acknowledgement for founding the County's Supporters' Association, but certainly it was Mike Green who "sowed the seeds" which, when harvested, produced such a rich crop. It is right therefore that he is remembered in this con-

G. Dews. Spectators of an earlier era saw in George Dews something of faithful Dick Pearson and, for today's spectators, there is much of Dews' play to be seen in Ted Hemsley's cricket. Dews joined the County in 1946 (having encountered Capt. A.F.T. White during his army service) and in sixteen seasons he scored nearly 17,000 runs with his attractive, attacking stroke play. He was a superb out-fielder, one of the best to have worn the County colours, and a very safe catcher. Only Roy Booth and Hugo Yarnold (and they were wicket-keepers!) and Dick Richardson have caught more than Dews who pouched 350 catches for the County. Dews' value to Worcestershire far exceeded his results for his sporting manner and dedicated but modest approach made him a firm favourite. He also played soccer for Middlesborough and Plymouth Argyle.

text for, over the years, the Supporters' Association has contributed generously to the County Cricket Club by providing and improving facilities at the Ground (for spectators and players), through important and essential financial support, and by its keen encouragement of the Club and its players. Since its formation in 1951 the Association has contributed well over £350,000 to the Club. If a visitor to the County Ground in 1899 was able to return today he would feel very much at home for the Ground retains much of the character and charm of the 19th century. The Pavilion and dressing rooms have been improved, seating for 5000 spectators provided, and a Dining Room and covered stand erected at the New Road end; there is a new Score Board and Press Box, accommodation has been provided for the office staff (previously a tin hut sufficed for the summer months after which the

Brigadier M.A. Green. Mike Green was appointed County Secretary immediately after the War and straightaway provided a keen and inspiring lead. Membership was improved and then maintained, and many ground improvements (including spectator accommodation) were undertaken. Perhaps Green's most important role was in mooting the idea of an organisation for the County's supporters.

Brigadier Green previously had played for Gloucestershire, and during his stay with the County he managed M.C.C. (England) tours to Australia and S. Africa.

The Supporters' Association, founded in June 1951 following an open air meeting held at the County Ground and addressed by Sir William Tennant, Lord Lieutenant of Worcestershire, has given immense help to the County and to cricket in the County in the three decades of its life.

nought. Hutton suffered the same fate in his second innings – b. Perks 0.

(a) The new scoreboard presented by the Supporters' Association in 1954, unveiled by Maurice Jewell, President of the County Club, whilst Ald. H. Morris, Chairman of the Supporters' Association looks on.

(b) The old scoreboard was situated at mid-wicket on the east side of the ground. The score shown here, 0 – 2, occurred during Yorkshire's first innings against the County in 1949, when Perks had bowled Len Hutton for

The Supporters' Association has always taken a keen interest in the County's players, particularly the young players. Here Ken Mills, Chairman, and Bob Brookes, Hon. Treasurer, present Phillip Neale with his Young Player of the Month award in May 1977 whilst Roy Booth, chairman of the County's Cricket Committee looks on.

73

The County Ground in Winter dress. (a) The floods. These pictures of the 1972 flood show the extent to which the ground floods. The flood water flows on to the ground from the west side (farthest from the river) as the ditches back-fill when the River Severn exceeds its summer level. The highest recorded flood was in 1947. A brass plaque level with the top of the bar in the Pavilion shows the depth of water that year.

(b) Winter Sport. On the rare occasions when flood water freezes over it is a signal for the hardy to pursue sport other than cricket. Ice-skating adds to the list of sports: bowls, tennis, cycling, athletics – and cricket, which have been played at New Road.

This "customary" view of the County Ground in 1902 differs little from the vista today. H.K. Foster and the Australian batsman Victor Trumper add grace and interest to a delightful and oft-repeated picture.

staff – both of them! – encamped for the winter to temporary but drier offices in the city centre), but the Ground still retains the atmosphere and appearance which is as well-known to all who have visited New Road as it is to the readers of "The Times" which, for many seasons carried a picture of the County Ground at Worcester as a sign that the cricket season – and summer – had begun and there was not too much wrong with the world!

Over the years the Committee of the Club has been conscious of the great heritage they have been entrusted with in the County Ground which has a unique and cherished place in the world of cricket. Doubtless Mike Green, his successors, and the Committees of the Supporters' Association could not have envisaged that, within a quarter of a century, the Club would be able to buy from the Dean and Chapter of Worcester Cathedral the freehold of the County Ground. This magnificent achievement was the culmination of some patient negotiations in 1976 which were carried out in a friendly and benevolent atmosphere which has so characterised the relationships between the Dean and Chapter and the Club ever since the Club became tenants of the farmland at New Road in 1896. Even this achievement was possible only

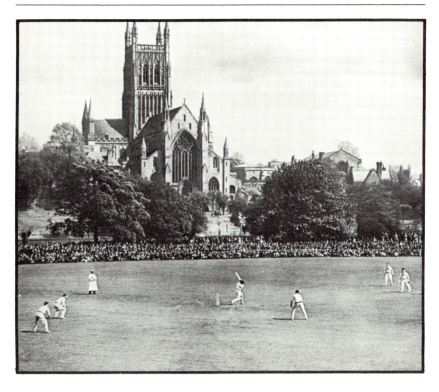

Bradman at Worcester, 1938. This picture, in addition to capturing The Don during his innings of 258, shows the County's reputed largest crowd which was reported as 14,000 spectators, many of whom paid 10/- (50p) to *stand* to see runs flow from the Australian's broad bat.

through the great generosity of the Supporters' Association who, with donations from individual County Members, provided the largest part of the purchase price of the County Ground. Thereby they played a part in securing the future of the County Cricket Club and they more than did justice to the scheme formulated by Mike Green and established by his colleagues who were the first officers of the Association.

Whilst referring to the County Ground in this chapter we must not forget that the idyllic Worcestershire cricket scene is not the only scene for which the Ground is famed. Its appearance in winter, several feet deep in Severn water, is almost as widely known.

When the subject of flooding crops up it is difficult to separate fact from fiction. Many of the older generation insist that the floods were good for the pitch. That might well have been so in earlier years but the amount of silt, detergent, and other muck (even occasional oil slicks) carried in floods today is not at all helpful.

The presence of a flood can be an embarrassment for the County Secretary who will be reminded (without fail!) that one of his predecessors, a clerical gentleman, is said (by whom is never revealed) to have swam across the Ground during a flood to retrieve some records kept in the score-box. (How, or if, he got those records back in any state of usefulness also is never revealed).

More unlikely, but it does come from "the horse's mouth", is Fred Hunt's tale of using the cricket nets to catch a 45lb salmon trapped in the boundary railings as a flood receded. Hunt's words seemed to recall the taste of that monster delicacy!

What other County Ground can tell of providing facilities for cricketers, bowls players, canoeists and salmon fishers? – and yet providing one of the most attractive of cricket grounds.

Mike Green's role in giving a clear, administrative lead was followed by Joe Lister, who was appointed Assistant Secretary to Major Bryan Bagly in 1954, became Joint Secretary with Peter Richardson for two years and, from 1958 until 1971 was Secretary of the Club in his own right. Lister also played in the County XI and later was to have a most

J. Lister, Worcestershire's Secretary from 1956 to 1971. Good enough to play first-class cricket for the County Lister's important cricketing contribution lay in the development of the young Second XI players who, under his captaincy, gained the experience which made them valuable members of the County XI of the Sixties. He was too a most capable and efficient Secretary and, as the County's longest-serving Secretary, it was wholly appropriate that he was at the administrative helm at the time Worcestershire advanced to its most successful era.

Second XI 1962, winners of the Second XI Championship. Standing (L to R): A. Ross-Slater (Hon. Scorer), J.W. Elliott, W. Davis, F.E. Rumsey, M. Downes, P.J. Robinson, K. Arch, E.J.O. Hemsley, C. Hallows (Coach)
Seated: R. Tattersall, R.G.M. Carter, R.J. Devereux, J. Lister (Captain), D.N.F. Slade, C.D. Fearnley, J.A. Ormrod.

important influence over the development of the Club's young cricketers and its playing policy as Captain of the Second XI. Under his captaincy Worcestershire II won the Second XI Championship in 1962 and 1963.

Joe Lister's Secretaryship, the longest in the Club's history, was to coincide with Don Kenyon's reign as County Captain which began when he succeeded Peter Richardson in 1958. Together these men were to lead the County to its first ever successes, in the 1960s.

Having been outsiders for so many years the County was now about to achieve its first real success and, having tasted the fruits of victory, it was to repeat that success at intervals through the next two decades.

Before we look more closely at "the Championship era" it is right that we remember the struggles, the loyalty, the joyful cricket played despite frustrations and set-backs and, above all, the continuing faith (as well as hope and charity!) of the earlier generations of Worcestershire's cricketers and their supporters. They all played a part on the pathway to this finally-achieved success. They must be allowed their rightful share in the triumphs of the Sixties and Seventies.

Champions At Last
1959 – 1979

For nearly sixty years Worcestershire had been playing County cricket, although there was little to show for it in the trophy cupboard. Indeed, there was *nothing* to show, despite a runners-up place in 1907 and a third in 1949.

Now at the end of the Fifties came a period of settled captaincy. Don Kenyon was at the helm in 1959 and was to be so for almost ten years. Perhaps, at first, not an obvious choice Kenyon became one of the great captains. One of the boys, but able to stand aloof from them when necessary (an asset for any good Captain), Kenyon gave the County a clear and determined lead. His prowess as a courageous opening batsman who sought straightaway to dominate and devastate opposing bowlers was never in question, and certainly there have not been many who have played some of the fastest bowlers so regularly, so convincingly and so successfully. Highly regarded as a player, and respected as a man, Kenyon was to captain a Champion County.

Success was not immediately forthcoming and in the first two seasons the County occupied places in the Championship table with which they had become all too familiar but then in 1961 came the improvement to fourth place. Worcestershire was now in areas it had only visited twice before. From that point, indeed for six of the nine seasons of Kenyon's captaincy, the County was to occupy one of the top five places in the table.

And for two of them Worcestershire was to be the Champion County.

Gradually the stalwarts of the immediate post-war decade gave way to younger aspirants. Yarnold, at the end of his career Worcestershire's most successful wicket-keeper, had been replaced by Roy Booth who was to succeed him for that title and who had joined the County in 1958 after having been on the staff at Yorkshire, his native county. The immaculate Booth was to prove a very worthy successor to a skilful and popular 'keeper.

Len Coldwell was now in harness with Jack Flavell and what an awesome pair they proved to be on the field; one cool, almost clockwork in his smooth, fluent bowling action, the other more workmanlike but fiery and venomous. The way in which they treated a cricket ball

D. Kenyon, one of Worcestershire's greatest cricketers. Don Kenyon, in his earliest years with the County was a slender young man on the taller side of medium height, with darkish fair hair and a healthy complexion. He matured into a well-built man, strong in the forearms, sharp of eye, with the keenest of cricket brains and that well-known ruddy countenance that typifies the successful countryman, for that is the appearance Kenyon creates. He was to become the County's most prolific batsman. A magnificent timer of the ball, he punched the ball through the covers with glorious cover drives, timed the ball sweetly off his legs, and unleashed a square drive which left fielders motionless. By no means an athletic fielder he was, however, a sound outfielder with a good arm, and a safe catcher.

perhaps gives an insight into their respective temperaments. Coldwell was a great polisher of the ball. As soon as the ball was 'dead' he wanted it in his hands and all the way back to his marker he would be polishing the ball. A little bit of saliva or sweat, plenty of elbow grease and flannel and, at the end of the over, the ball would be like new. To see the grass trapped in the stitching would tell how frequently the ball hit the seam. Jack seldom seemed to polish the ball. If he had the ball in his hand at the start of his run-up that was sufficient. He knew what he wanted to do to the batsman at the other end and the ball, coupled with his skill, great 'heart' and fiery determination, was his means of achieving that.

A battery of third seamers backed up the fine opening pair. Schoolmaster (in fact and appearance and now one of our national cricket coaches) Bob Carter was the senior of these, Jim Standen the most effervescent and the most consistently successful, Brian Brain

H. Yarnold. Hugo Yarnold was one of the few Worcestershire-born men to keep wicket for the County, and what a skilled craftsman he was. He was a sound, smart rather than brilliant, wicket-keeper who maintained splendidly consistent form season in, season out. He was adept at dealing with all bowled at him but in an era when spin bowlers were more plentiful he spent much time standing up to the stumps. Later in his career he suffered problems with his knee and had a knee-cap removed to resolve the problems. On the field a foam-backed pad gave added protection, off the field a leg caliper took some of the strain, but through it all his courage ensured there was no falling off in his value to the side. Against Scotland in 1951 he created a world record of six stumpings in an innings (and took a catch as well!). Two seasons earlier he had performed the rare feat of capturing 110 victims in the season. In all he held 456 catches and made 228 stumpings for the County. After his County career, spanning the years 1938–1955, had ended he became a County umpire (and stood in 3 Tests) and it was whilst returning home from a match in 1974 that he was killed in a car accident.

perhaps the most talented when in the right frame of mind.

If the Captain had a full armoury of fast bowlers his slow-bowling was not noticeably weak. Martin Horton was still taking wickets with his off-spin as well as opening the batting with Kenyon, and Doug Slade was a slow left-arm spinner in the classical mould (like Dick Howorth before him not a great spinner of the ball, but a smooth action provided great control of line and length). Norman Gifford, a Lancastrian who

L.J. Coldwell. Len Coldwell arrived late for his Worcestershire trial covered in cuts and abrasions as a result of an accident sustained en route from Devon. He promptly bowled out some of the senior batsmen including Don Kenyon (and claims he did not know it was Kenyon), which augured well for his future. Perhaps he should also have taken greater note of the injuries for he was to suffer throughout his career with leg and back injuries. Despite those injuries he was a most successful bowler, and he took over 1000 wickets for the County in the seasons 1955 to 1969.

With a smooth economical run to the wicket he bowled, from a tall position, at a lively, right-arm fast-medium pace. His stock delivery was the in-swinger but it moved disconcertingly late, and was varied with the occasional one going the other way. Accuracy and variety of pace were also important parts of his armoury in which the well-disguised slower ball and a faster delivery were valuable weapons.

Len Coldwell was a delightful and courageous cricketer and a master craftsman bowler for the County. On his retirement in 1969 he returned to his native Devon where, in his leisure moments, he now hammers a golf ball unmercifully.

J.A. Flavell. Jack Flavell had played little serious cricket when he first came to the County's notice. In his younger days as a fiery, red-headed bowler he lacked accuracy and was only moderately successful. Then, in 1957, he took 100 wickets for the first time and barely looked back from then on.

He was a strong, devastating, and great-hearted bowler whose sole aim was to attack the stumps. This he did to great effect. In 1961 he headed the national averages with 171 wickets at 17.79 runs each. He played a most vital role in retaining the Championship in 1965. In the County's late run of wins there came the "Flavell five" – five matches won between August 8th and 25th with "Flav." taking 46 wickets. That was superb bowling and typical of his heart, strength and tenacity. Like Len Coldwell he too suffered injuries from which others, less determined, might not have returned to the game. With Coldwell he formed one of the most successful and least relished bowling partnerships in the game. A great family man away from the game, Jack Flavell is a keen golfer and gardener, and a successful restaurateur.

had opted for Worcestershire in preference to his native County, also was a left-arm spinner but of a different style. He too had command of length and line, but imparted greater spin to the ball and, whilst varying his pace, bowled naturally faster than the 'classical' left-armers. On wickets which offered any encouragement he was almost unplayable.

To back up the bowlers there were some peerless close catchers. Dick Richardson, Gifford, Slade and Ron Headley, who was just making his way as an attacking left-hand bat, ensured that few catches went begging.

D.N.F. Slade. Pictured here, in 1968, with Worcestershire's newest recruit, Glenn Turner, and Bob Carter is Doug Slade, a valuable member of the County team during the Sixties. In his first-class career he took over 500 wickets. He bowled frequently in a left-arm spin combination with Gifford, and they were complemented by Horton's off-spinners. His doughty batting advanced and he was a member of that select group of Worcestershire's admirable and safe close catchers. After leaving County cricket he played for Shropshire C.C.C., and for West Bromwich Dartmouth in the Birmingham League, and has been a major influence in the improved fortunes of Worcester City C.C. in local cricket. It was Slade too who coached Dipak Patel and recommended him to the County.

On the batting front Kenyon and Horton were consistent and prolific openers; Dick Richardson, a free stroke player, was good enough to be selected for England; and Headley had the quick eye and natural athleticism of a West Indian. If icing was required on this rich cake it came in the form of T.W. Graveney. Formerly with Gloucestershire (who did not share his views about the captaincy of that County) Tom Graveney joined neighbouring Worcestershire. He was required to qualify for his adopted County and spent that qualifying season playing Second XI and Birmingham League cricket (with an occasional Tourist or University match added to whet the appetite).

When he rejoined the County circuit it was a more purposeful

Graveney that spectators saw. The classical grace and timing were still there and, to this grace was added a steel-like dimension, so that under Kenyon's leadership T.W.G. was to score runs a-plenty for Worcestershire and, again, for England.

A team that included Kenyon, Horton, Graveney, Headley, Richardson (D.W.), Booth, Slade, Gifford, Carter (or Standen or Brain), Coldwell and Flavell could not but provide entertaining and successful cricket.

To give support when England, or injury, required the attentions of senior players there was Alan Ormrod, thought to be another Graveney

---

Quartet of Bowlers, 1961.		
M.J. Horton	L.J. Coldwell	It is interesting to compare these figures with those achieved by the "hundred wicket" quartet of 1937. Coincidentally, both quartets were comprised of two fast-medium right-arm bowlers, a left-arm spinner and an off-spinner.
101 wkts	140 wkts	
Av. 21.64	Av. 19.25	
N. Gifford	J.A. Flavell	
133 wkts	171 wkts	
Av. 19.66	Av. 17.79	

M.J. Horton. 18,000 runs, 774 wickets and 149 catches in fifteen seasons constitutes a prodigious all-round effort. These were the results of Martin Horton's endeavours for the County which he joined in 1949 at the age of 15. His early years were interrupted by National Service but in his first full season, 1955, he achieved the double. As a gritty right-hand batsman with an equable temperament his promotion to open the innings with Kenyon brought the best from him and provided the County with a prolific opening partnership. He was a strong on-driver and he had a rapier-like square cut. As an off-spinner he pushed the ball through and bowled "tight" and it was primarily as a bowler who could bat that he played for England in 1959. With Ted Arnold and Dick Howorth, Horton is one of the County's most prolific all-rounders. After retiring from County cricket he became National Coach to New Zealand.

in the making, and Duncan Fearnley, whose command of Second XI cricket was never quite translated to the first-class game.

Off the field the players were supported by a worthy team. Sir George Dowty, a true (and successful) son of Worcestershire, provided drive and determination as President; Gilbert Ashton, himself a Worcestershire player, was now Chairman of the Club, and with his old world courtesy and charm and his ability and desire to seek the best in everyone was also a "champion" leader. The players had a high regard too for Hon. Richard Lygon, chairman of the Cricket Committee. Joe Lister was an efficient and imperturbable Secretary.

Also part of "the team" were the County Coach, Charlie Hallows, Bill Powell, the masseur, who looked after his charges as a mother hen looks after her chicks, and the aptly named Hon. Scorer, Bill Faithful.

D.W. Richardson. Dick Richardson as a cricketer was something of an enigma, but what an attractive and delightful enigma. When Worcestershire scored freely Richardson, paradoxically, was often unsuccessful; when the side was in trouble his combative and indomitable spirit showed. In the dressing rooms it was said that his brother Peter had five strokes but only ever played three, whilst Dick had six shots and always played eight! There was much of the cavalier in his cricket.

Quick on his feet, and with a natural gift of timing, Richardson showed the left-hander's panache in his off-driving. He was a strong leg-side player but could cut with wristy grace.

In all he scored nearly 16,000 runs for Worcestershire and yet he is best remembered for the brilliance and near infallibility of his close-catching. No other Worcestershire player has caught more than his 412 catches for the County, and there have been few, if any, better catchers in the game.

87

R.G.A. Headley. To be the "son of a famous father" can, at time, be a considerable handicap but it is not one which daunted Ron Headley whose father, George, was one of the best of West Indian cricketers. Ron Headley made his Worcestershire debut in 1958 and by his all too early retirement in 1974 he had scored 20,712 runs for the County; and taken 340 catches. He was a fine attacking bat and there was a formidable and exciting ferocity about his driving, particularly in his straight driving. An effervescent cricketer, he took the attack to the bowlers and sought, usually successfully, to dominate them from the start. His best season was in 1961 when he scored over 2000 runs. In 1973 he played for the W. Indies against England. As a close catcher he ranks with the best of the County's coterie of catchers and he was also an able attacking fielder away from the bat where he prowled with the menace of a panther.

A champion team to bring the County Championship to Worcestershire, and bring it they did – in 1964.

That season Worcestershire and neighbouring Warwickshire set such a blistering pace in the County Championship that very few other Counties were ever in contention. The County had drawn the home match with Warwickshire and then, in mid July, a win was achieved at Edgbaston when Warwickshire was bowled out for 72 and 86. That was the quality Champions are made of but the County, so unused to the heady heights they now found themselves in, had to wait five weeks until their victory over Gloucestershire (and the result of the Hampshire v. Warwickshire match) for the Championship to be a mathematical certainty.

T.W. Graveney. Wet weather diversions for young boys, and journalists, often include selecting an all-time World XI or England XI. Even to be considered for such a team must rank as a great compliment; to be regularly included in such lists is the mark of true greatness. Tom Graveney has that distinction. His too was a genius for run-making, both in the volume of runs he scored and more so in the exquisite way in which those runs were scored.

Graveney was a front-foot player, even to the extent of being able to pull or hook (on the rare occasions he was so tested) off the front foot. His hallmark, in a full array of elegant strokes, was the cover drive. In ten seasons (from 1961) for his adopted County he scored 13,160 at an average of 46.02 but in a first-class career which had started thirteen years earlier his career aggregate was not far short of 50,000 runs.

The tall, genial right-hander never took his art for granted and each day during the season he was to be seen in the nets. It was a part of his game, and one which easily could be emulated; the pure genius of his batting cannot be emulated. He was awarded the O.B.E. in 1968 to mark his services to the game.

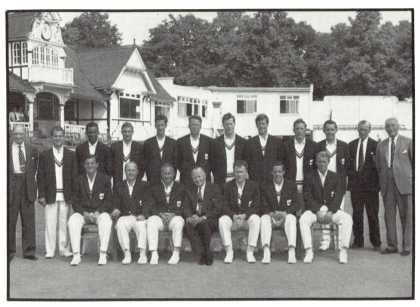

County Champions 1964. The County had been playing County Championship cricket for sixty-five years when the players pictured above achieved what so many of their predecessors had strived for, played for, and dreamed of for so many years. County Champions at last.

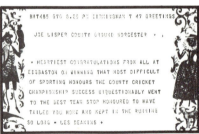

A celebration fit for Champions. Don Kenyon and his team celebrate. Dress: informal.

County Champions for the first time. For everyone involved this was an immense thrill, and many inside and outside the County's boundaries joined in the congratulations, the unbounded pleasure, and the celebrations. We should not forget those who through the years of the Club's life had worked for this success; particularly those associated with the Club during the lean period between the Wars when even the prospect of a win must have seemed miraculous, and also those who immediately prior to the Great War wondered if Worcestershire would long survive in first-class cricket.

Some fairy tales, just occasionally, do come true and when at the start of the 1965 season Joe Lister ceremoniously unfurled over the County Ground the County Champions pennant (presented each year by the previous holders to the new champions) the previous season's success must still have seemed a dream.

For that Championship win to be repeated in 1965, the Club's centenary year, was indeed a fairy story come true. Worcestershire retained the Championship after 100 years of existence as a County Cricket Club. The battle was a little harder than in the previous season and, after a poor start, only a late run of eleven wins enabled the Champions pennant to remain rightly at New Road.

Ninety-eight years in the wilderness and then two successive years of triumph. It was almost too much!

The side had changed little since the previous year. Indeed the only significant change was the addition of B.L. D'Oliveira, the Cape-coloured South African all-rounder. Denied any serious cricket by his country's apartheid policy, Basil D'Oliveira had come to play league cricket in England in 1961 to gain experience that would enable him to help his fellow cricketers at home. His contribution to the game of cricket was to be unique and, perhaps, time will tell that this contribution was far greater than the vast deeds he achieved on the field. In his first year in County cricket (having like Graveney qualified for Worcestershire by playing Second XI and Birmingham League cricket), at the age of 33, D'Oliveira proved himself worthy to be a member of the Champion County.

In 1963 the Gillette Cup was inaugurated, a one-day limited over knock-out competition, which was to prove tremendously popular with players and spectators and to be the fore-runner of the John Player League (introduced in 1969) and the Benson and Hedges Cup (in 1972).

Worcestershire created history by being Finalists, with Sussex, in the first year of the Gillette Cup and Norman Gifford was Man of the Match in that first Cup Final at Lord's. Three seasons later, in 1966,

B.L. D'Oliveira. At the age of thirty-three Basil D'Oliveira came to England to accept a once-in-a-lifetime chance to further his cricket, with a professional engagement for Middleton in the Lancashire League. In that wet Lancashire April of 1961 he first encountered grass pitches, having played his cricket in S. Africa on matting stretched out on gravel. Within three summers his wildest dream had been fulfilled and he had become a County cricketer, with Worcestershire. By 1966, and at an age when many players are finishing Test cricket, he embarked on a Test career that was to span 44 Test Matches.

Throughout all these novel experiences, including the disappointing and distressing period when the 1968-69 England tour to S. Africa was banned because of his inclusion in the party, he has remained calm, dignified, and abundantly grateful to a game which had offered him so much. It is those characteristics which endeared him to so many people within and beyond the frontiers of sport.

A natural competitor prepared to back his ability against any of his opponents D'Oliveira is a most accomplished bat whose best innings often have been played at a time of crisis for Worcestershire or for England. Despite a short back lift his powerful fore-arms enable him to hit the ball extremely hard. He is a courageous and outstanding puller and cutter, and drives through the covers and mid-wicket with great force. His apparently gentle medium-pace swing bowling has gained him many valuable wickets and the economy of his bowling has been advantageous in one-day cricket.

In 1969 this fine cricketer was honoured with the award of the O.B.E.

Don Kenyon – of the serene, unruffable temperament, the magnificent repertoire of strokes, and the bat which – to bowlers, at least – seemed to be the broadest in County cricket, continued throughout his career to score prodigiously for the County. By 1967 when he retired he had made more runs and scored more centuries for the County than any other player; fewer than two dozen men in the history of the game have scored more runs than Kenyon.

The captaincy almost was thrust upon him in 1959 and his earliest seasons at the helm cannot have been easy for him. His good sense, natural dignity and shrewd cricket brain enabled him to grow in authority and to become one of the most successful and best-respected captains of the post-war era. If neither County nor player had expected his elevation to the captaincy, Dame Fate played a bold stroke which set Worcestershire on the path to a first Championship and which provided Kenyon with a permanent niche in Worcestershire's history.

the County again reached the Final and yet again were unsuccessful, on this occasion losing to Warwickshire in an all-Midlands Final.

Hereabouts Kenyon's team began to break up. Horton left in 1966 to become New Zealand's National Coach, and Kenyon, Flavell and Dick Richardson retired a season later to be followed, in 1969, by Coldwell who returned to his native Devon. They had given valiant service to the County, between them giving the County an aggregate service of 86 years. They had carved for themselves a permanent place in the County's history as Champion cricketers.

J.A. Ormrod. Alan Ormrod, Worcestershire's Scottish Lancastrian, joined the County in 1960, aged seventeen, and made his debut two seasons later. His batting has always borne the grace and mark of a class player but it was not until 1965, when he played a valuable part in the retaining of the Championship, that he began to establish himself. From then on his progress was gradual until, in 1975, when he became Glenn Turner's regular opening partner, the very best of Ormrod was seen.

A composed, unruffled and technically correct batsman, he is an immensely attractive player in all he does. Now a high-class cricketer in his own right, there is much of Graveney in his classic style, particularly in his flowing cover driving, and no praise could be higher. It remains a mystery why his sound technique, calm approach, and honest endeavour have not gained him a chance at higher levels for others much less equipped have been so rewarded. His batting is complemented by his safe fielding close to the bat, especially at slip, and he is the loyalest of team men.

G.M. Turner. Glenn Turner came to England (after working on the night shift in a Dunedin bakery to raise the fare) for trials with Warwickshire who subsequently could not offer him a place on the staff. Arrangements were made for him to have a trial with Worcestershire before going on to Lancashire. Don Kenyon and Tom Graveney saw enough for Turner's journey north to be unnecessary.

At first Worcestershire appeared to have gained a dour, defensive, right-handed batsman. With increasing experience came confidence and a clearer awareness of the requirements of the game, and then blossomed the world-class batting skills so efficiently and prodigiously displayed in recent seasons. Ten centuries in 1970, 1000 runs by the end of May in 1973, the highest run-scorer in the world during the Seventies, leading run-scorer in John Player League cricket and the holder of many of Worcestershire's batting records are but a handful of Turner's achievements.

His batting style is his own. Neat in appearance, light and well-balanced on his feet, this slimly built player is an immaculate timer of the ball. The bat is held in an unusual "back-of-the-handle" grip. The high, but not exaggerated, backlift enables the bat to flow through into field-piercing drives, savage cuts, or the well-timed shot off his legs through mid-wicket.

In the field he is a safe slip catcher and a free-moving, swooping outfielder with an uncannily accurate arm.

Don Kenyon too had created for himself a special place in Worcestershire's history as the Captain of the County's Championship side. His batting alone would have achieved him that special regard as his is the largest aggregate ever scored *for Worcestershire*. Statistics however do not give the full picture of Kenyon's importance to his team for his forthright style and his ability to dominate the opposition frequently paved the way for later batsmen to continue in similar vein. It is as Captain however that he will be best remembered; a calm, unperturbable, but determined leader and, above all, highly successful. When his playing days were over he continued to bring to the game his vast experience both as a Test Selector, member of the County Committee and sometime Chairman of its Cricket Committee.

Tom Graveney succeeded Kenyon and he had the difficult task not only of following the County's most successful Captain but also of bringing along the players of the new generation. Amongst these Alan Ormrod was establishing himself as a class player, a status he confirmed more emphatically when he became the County's regular opening partner with Glenn Turner following Ron Headley's too early departure at the end of the 1974 season. Headley and Turner had proved capable successors to Kenyon and Horton. Headley's bright and attacking approach to opening the innings was forthright, much like Kenyon's. Turner, in contrast, was more circumspect in his earlier years but as each season passed by he confirmed his world-class ranking.

Another Commonwealth player, Vanburn Holder of Barbados and the West Indies, had joined the County, on Graveney's recommendation in 1968. He quickly proved himself to be a fast bowler whose great control and accuracy made him a formidable player. It is useful to consider Holder as being typical in the context of overseas-born players who play County cricket during the English cricket season and then return home to continue playing there. Holder, by the end of the 1979 season and at the age of 34, will thus have played almost 25 *consecutive* cricket seasons. That is a great deal of cricket, and even more so for a fast bowler with over 40 Test appearances to his name.

Although the County had gained a new fast bowler in 1968 it lost the services of another grand cricketer at the end of the summer when Roy Booth decided to put away his 'keeper's gloves. Booth, in a career with Worcestershire which spanned the years 1956 to 1970, was "a good County cricketer" – and a mighty fine 'keeper. Immaculate in appearance and in style and remarkably consistent behind the stumps, he captured over 1000 victims for the County and twice took 100 or more victims in the season. He, too, when his playing days were over continued to give equally conscientious service to the Club as a member of Committee; and is the current Chairman of the Cricket Committee.

Carter (or Brain) and Holder had by now succeeded Flavell and Coldwell; spin came from the left-armers Slade and Gifford, and Standen was still a useful third-seamer or medium-fast opening bowler when footballing commitments with West Ham United allowed. Worcestershire seem to have had a preponderance of footballing cricketers over the years. For other Counties Denis Compton and Arthur Milton stand out as footballing cricketers, but alongside Standen in the Worcestershire team in the late Sixties there was Ted Hemsley (Shrewsbury

V.A. Holder in action. Worcestershire's gentle giant of a fast bowler joined the County in April 1968 having impressed Tom Graveney against whom he bowled when the latter was visiting the W. Indies several months earlier. Holder has been the County's main strike bowler ever since. Tall and lean of frame, he bowls at a lively right-arm fast-medium pace, and is capable of bowling (without signalling it to the world) a genuinely fast delivery. His great strength is the immaculate control with which he bowls, the batsman seldom being allowed a moment's respite. His long curving run, with its loping early strides gradually giving way to a smooth approach to the wicket, culminates in a naturally lithe and unstressed bowling action.

In the outfield he covers the ground with surprising speed and he has a powerful arm. His batting is almost characterised by two shots: a stroke, usually defensive, played off a far-outstretched front foot, and the shot played off the back foot with which the ball, after a flourishing "wind up" of a back lift, is hammered many a mile and in a variety of directions but quite often straight. He has scored a first-class century (for Barbados) and is the only Worcestershire bowler to have taken 100 Test Match wickets.

Town, Sheffield United and Doncaster Rovers) later to be joined by Jim Cumbes (a goalkeeper successively for Runcorn Town, Tranmere Rovers, West Bromwich Albion, Aston Villa, Coventry City, Southport, Portland Timbers and Worcester City) and Phil Neale (Lincoln City). In earlier seasons there had been George Dews (Middlesborough), Victor Fox (Middlesborough and Wolves), and even as far back as G.F. Wheldon (Aston Villa) who played for the County at the start of the century the County seems to have attracted more than its share of footballing cricketers.

Graveney retired from the County game in 1970. Truly he had graced the game as a man and as a great cricketer, indeed one of the greatest of all batsmen. If he had never scored a run the splendour and grace of his batting would have provided entertainment enough but his genius – and it was pure art – was allied to a remarkable proficiency which made him a copious – and stylish – scorer of runs.

Gifford had been appointed to succeed Graveney as skipper and in his first season he was recalled to the England Test team and also led Worcestershire to the top of the table. On this occasion it was the top of the John Player League table. The Sunday afternoon 40-overs game, whilst it may still be an anathema to some 'traditionist' spectators, has done much to re-stimulate cricket interest among spectators and has encouraged batsmen to play (or invent!) more scoring strokes, bowlers to bowl more accurately and economically and, above all, has made fielding a brilliantly athletic spectacle.

The County's success in the competition that season was by a hair's breadth or, more accurately, by three decimal places, for Worcestershire ended the season level with Essex on points but took the title on faster scoring rate by 0.003 runs/ball. However narrow they are, championships are championships, and all those who witnessed the vital match at Dudley against Warwickshire, and Ron Headley's calculated, courageous batting that day will believe the J.P.L. title was justly earned.

Gifford's team was to achieve further one-day successes in 1973 and in 1976 when the County again went to Lord's for a Cup Final, on both occasions unsuccessfully, for the Final of the Benson and Hedges Cup.

By now a burly right-arm fast-medium bowler, John Inchmore, had joined the County from Northumberland; Jim Cumbes, previously with Lancashire and Surrey and now increasingly available as his football commitments diminished; and a local product, Paul Pridgeon, were the fast bowlers supporting Holder. D'Oliveira could bowl off-spinners when the wickets were more suited to this than his more usual medium-

Third Seamers. For a number of seasons following Reg Perks' retirement Flavell and Coldwell formed the only *regular partnership* of opening bowlers. Others shared the new ball with them from time to time but more often than not played a valuable supporting role as third seamers to this pair. A number of fast-medium bowlers were tried by the County including J. Aldridge, K. Lobban, D.B. Pearson, F.E. Rumsey (before his move to Somerset). Aldridge was the most successful of these. (a) John

(b)

wicket he delivered the ball with a whip-like action which generated surprising pace from one of such slender build. He joined the County originally in 1958 and, during a twice interrupted career which extended to 1975, he took 508 wickets.

(a)

Aldridge, known to his cricketing friends as "Long John", took 241 wickets for the County between 1956 and 1960. A tall, lean man he bowled from a considerable height after a long run to the wicket. He was a fiery bowler who gained pace and bounce from his height.

(b) Brian Brain, a bowler of considerable natural ability, arguably was the most talented of this quartet of bowlers. Thin as a lath and with a smooth economical approach to the

(c)

(c) Jim Standen was one of Worcestershire's footballing cricketers. An enthusiastic and lively right-arm medium-paced bowler, Standen took more than 300 wickets for the County in twelve seasons, and would have taken many more but for the demands of soccer which restricted his cricket to a short spell each summer. He was a valuable member of the Championship team in 1964, and headed the first-class bowling averages that season. His excellent fielding reflected his extrovert personality. 1964 was a notable year for Standen as, apart from his part in the County's Championship success, he had kept goal for West Ham United in their Cup Final win in the Spring of that year.

(d)

(d) Bob Carter was a great-hearted, genial cricketer. A lively right-arm fast-medium bowler he bowled with immense commitment. Whether it was for him a good day or a bad day he gave nothing less than 100% in effort and never complained about when or what he was expected to bowl. In twelve seasons he took more than 520 wickets for the County, and he was a valuable member of the Championship teams of 1964 and 1965 and also of the 1971 team which won the John Player League. He is now one of cricket's National Coaches.

Footballing cricketers today.

(a)

(a) Ted Hemsley's life is the envy of many. Since leaving Bridgnorth Grammar School he has played professional sport: soccer in the winter for Shrewsbury town, Sheffield United and Doncaster Rovers, and cricket in the summer for Worcestershire. Hemsley's approach to batting is uninhibited and he relishes scoring at a spanking rate. If the side requires quick runs he is prepared to go for them and whilst this means that his innings may often be short and sweet it is not to deny that he is capable of making big scores (and making them attractively) or playing a gutsy knock when his side is in trouble. His right-arm medium-paced bowling is infrequently unveiled, but he is a superb all-round fielder.

pace bowling and furthermore he was especially economical in one-day games. The bowling relied heavily on Gifford who has proved to be a sound, competitive and much respected County Captain. His is leadership by example. If there is bowling to be done he will not shirk his

(b)

(b) Jim Cumbes shares much of the approach of his fellow footballers, Standen and Hemsley, and his fellow fast bowler, Bob Carter.

He is a cheerful cricketer whose whole-hearted contribution to team morale is as valuable as the wickets he takes. Cumbes bowls at a spritely medium pace derived from a full 'windmill' action which follows a modest, bounding run to the wicket. In earlier seasons he bowled with greater pace, but in recent years he has remodelled his action and although he bowls now at a gentler pace his accuracy is much improved.

In 1978, to the delight of many friends in and outside the game, he was awarded his County cap after sixteen seasons (or part seasons!) of County cricket with Lancashire, Surrey, Lancashire (again) and Worcestershire.

(c)

(c) Phillip Neale came to the County whilst still at school.

Following his university career (at Leeds, where he gained a degree in Russian) he joined Lincoln City F.C. for whom he still plays in the winter months.

A right-hand batsman of undoubted ability he was capped by the County in 1978. He is often a cautious and somewhat uncertain player at the start of his innings but a determined defence enables him to remain at the crease, and the longer he stays there the more attractive does his strokeplay become. As befits a dual athlete he is an exciting and capable outfielder.

R. Booth. Roy Booth's County cricket career started with Yorkshire. In true Yorkshire fashion it was decided to give Booth and fellow 'keeper' Jimmy Binks half a season each to stake a claim for a place in the County XI. Booth was given first opportunity but, by the arrangement, had to give way to Binks who retained his place. Booth came south to join Worcestershire in 1956 and was to become the County's best and most successful 'keeper'.

In all he took 868 catches for Worcestershire and stumped 147 batsmen. In two seasons, 1960 and 1964, he took 100 wickets. His batting was never overlooked and in three successive seasons, 1959 to 1961, he came very close to the rare achievement of the wicket-keeper's double of 1000 runs and 100 victims. He scored over 10,000 runs in first-class cricket.

As a wicket-keeper he was consistent year-in and year-out, exceedingly efficient, immaculate without being flamboyant, and a source of great confidence to his fellow players. His batting was characterised by a high back-lift which promised, and frequently produced, prodigious hitting, typically through mid-wicket. Among many innings those he is best remembered for are the one against Sussex in the first Gillette Cup Final in 1963 and another against Sussex which enabled the County to win the match and retain the Championship in 1965. A loyal and popular team man, Booth was a vital member of the Worcestershire team in the Sixties. Yorkshire's loss was a truly beneficial gain for Worcestershire.

---

share and certainly he is prepared to take the 'stick' (and save a young bowler) on those occasions when the ball is being hammered to all parts of the ground; if the fielding needs to be tight and aggressive (especially close to the wicket) he is there; and whilst he is not the most graceful or high scoring of batsmen he relishes a fight and does not easily give up his wicket.

His leadership brought its just rewards in 1974 when the County Championship was won for the third time, just ten years after the first major success had been achieved.

The County XI set off on its third Championship season like a greyhound out of a trap. By early July six out of eight County matches had been won. Then came a period of mixed fortunes which ended with an annihilating defeat by Hampshire, who were heading the Championship table. The character of Gifford's side was then clearly seen; despite these reverses they had not given up hope. Victories against Essex and Glamorgan, at home, and against Notts, at Newark, reduced Hampshire's lead to two points. Worcestershire went off to play Essex at Chelmsford whilst Hampshire entertained Yorkshire at Bournemouth – and a season which had started in drought conditions ended awash! However a break in the weather was sufficient for Worcestershire (mainly in the comfortable form of its Captain who took 7–15 in fourteen overs) to bowl out Essex. The four bowling bonus points gained were sufficient to take the County ahead of the frustrated, rain-bound, Hampshire players and to bring Worcestershire its third County Championship.

Rain may well have denied Hampshire a final opportunity to retain their title but there can be no doubt that the County's eleven wins during the season, its weathering of the mid-season reversals, and the fact that eighteen players were called on during the summer as a result of injuries, provided every justification for the title again to rest proudly at New Road. Shortly after the Championship was decided the County received a telegram from Hampshire's President, Ronnie Aird, with a warm tribute from a vanquished but sporting Club.

That same season Worcestershire also reached the quarter-finals of the Benson and Hedges Cup and the semi-finals of the Gillette Cup. It was a heady summer.

It can be argued that the County's performances are, at times, still inconsistent as, having acquired the taste for success, the County now seems to fluctuate between the top and the bottom of the various tables. The 1978 and 1979 seasons provide good examples of this. In 1978, apart from finishing fourth in the John Player League, the County performed badly in the other three competitions (Schweppes Championship, Gillette Cup and Benson and Hedges Cup). In 1979 with only one change in the playing staff (Younis Ahmed had joined the County, having been released by Surrey after 14 years at the Oval) the County were runners-up in the Schweppes Championship, third in the John Player League, and quarter-finalists in the Benson and Hedges competition.

A feature of the current Worcestershire side is the presence of young players such as Dipak Patel, at twenty an all-rounder of great promise who has already scored four first-class centuries; Phillip Neale, the most recent of the County's footballing cricketers who should be a regular 1000 runs a season man – and maybe an England player too; Stephen Henderson, as yet relatively inexperienced but a massive run-scorer in Second XI cricket; and the wicket-keeper batsman, David Humphries, who very easily could become the best in the country in that dual role. Loyal and valuable team men such as Cumbes and

N. Gifford. Norman Gifford applied to Worcestershire for a trial following the County's advertisement in The Cricketer for bowlers. His native Lancashire got to hear of his interest but Gifford chose Worcestershire as the pleasant, friendly atmosphere of the County had impressed him. He joined the staff in 1958 and made his debut two years later. That summer he headed the County's bowling averages and in the following summer, his first full season, he took 133 wickets and won his County cap.

Gifford is a fine left-arm spinner and match-winning bowler. No other Worcestershire bowler, apart from Reg Perks, has taken more than his 1565 wickets in first-class cricket. His natural bowling action delivers the ball slightly faster than the "classical" left-armer. As he also spins the ball more than most spinners he is an extremely difficult player to score off. Although there is a tendency to consider him as a 'flat' bowler he is more than capable of flighting the ball when required. He is equally capable of pushing the ball through and bowling into the 'block-hole' and, particularly in one-day matches, this enables him to tie batsmen down very effectively. As a tail-end batsman 'Giff' is a determined left-hander who has fought some splendid rearguard actions.

As County Captain he has proved to be a popular, shrewd and successful leader. He has given devoted and unstinting service to the Club, to England in fifteen Test Matches, and to cricket in general. The award to him of the M.B.E. for services to cricket was richly deserved.

Benson and Hedges Cup Finals. The County appeared in the Benson and Hedges Cup Finals in 1973 and '76. Here in '73 Norman Gifford receives his medal and the runners-up pennant whilst the victorious Kent players add their congratulations.

Holder are in an occupation where they could not be expected to go on for ever and a day, but the batsmen such as Turner, Ormrod, Younis and Hemsley have several good years cricket left in them.

As we have seen, the County often has been blessed with a good batting side or a team strong in bowling and it is only in the last twenty years or so that Worcestershire has had the good fortune to bring together a well-balanced team.

The well-balanced side has produced more consistent results, long and eagerly awaited triumphs, and a taste for success has been keenly developed.

A considerable measure of the credit for the improvement in the Club's fortunes justifiably can be shared by those who have served willingly and with conscientious devotion as members of the County's committees through the ages. All serve, or have served, because they could offer some specialist knowledge or experience to the management of Club affairs and, above all, because they share an unbounded interest in the well-being of Worcestershire County Cricket Club. Seldom in the limelight and rarely, if ever, seeking it the generations of Worcestershire's committees have experienced the varying pleasures and sense of fulfilment of working for the Club's more recent and highly-prized successes and, more important, in ensuring the Club's continued wellbeing and good health. All who share their concern for the Club's fortunes owe much to those who have given of themselves so freely for the good of Worcestershire County Cricket Club.

The County Club has also been well served by its staff through the years. Whilst it is invidious to mention by name some of those who have given outstanding service, an exception is made here to acknowledge their special contribution to the life of the Club. If Fred Hunt was a superb head Groundsman then in recent seasons two of his successors have been accorded similar recognition by their colleagues in the game. Gordon Prosser was nominated Watney Mann County Groundsman of the Year in 1972, 1973 and 1975 and his successor, Richard Stevens, received the Award in 1978. A splendid and exceptional example of loyal service to a County Cricket Club has been provided by Mrs Grace Fuller who joined Brigadier Green's staff in 1946 and is still with the

J.D. Inchmore. John Inchmore joined the County in 1973 following trials with both Worcestershire and Warwickshire. His impressive bowling for Stourbridge in the Birmingham League had attracted the attention of both counties, and ultimately he decided to join Worcestershire.

A tall, superbly built right-arm fast-medium bowler, Inchmore bowls with all-action determination. From the start of his run there exists an obvious desire and striving to get to the wicket and to bowl as quickly as he can let the ball go. Inchmore has the fire and venom expected of faster bowlers and sometimes, when things are not going just as he would wish, that venom mercurially is turned on himself. When he is "on song" he is a fine sight particularly for those in the field with him rather than those waiting to bat against him.

As a batsman he is more than capable and he has scored a cultured and attractive first-class hundred.

County Champions 1974.

D.N. Patel. Born in Kenya in 1958 Dipak Patel has lived in England since he was nine years old. At school in West Bromwich he displayed an interest in soccer which was later succeeded by his interest in cricket. Patel came to the notice of Doug Slade who coached him and recommended him to the County. His first real contact with Worcestershire was in 1975 when he played for the Second XI in his school holidays.

The following summer he joined the staff, made his debut and scored his maiden first-class century at the age of 17 years and 7 months. His batting is attractive, fluent and extremely graceful. As an off-spin bowler he has improved with experience and greater confidence so that, with his lithe fielding and good arm, he can be considered a genuine all-rounder. In 1979, and not yet twenty-one, he received his County cap.

Throughout its history Worcestershire County Cricket Club has been well served on and off the field. Reference has been made elsewhere to some of those who, in earlier days, worked behind the scenes. Pictured here are three more recent stalwarts.

(a)

(a) Gordon Prosser was Head Groundsman from 1970 to 1076. In that time he won the Watney Mann County Groundsman of the Year trophy (judged by umpires and County captains) three times in four years.

Inset is Cyril Hayes who was one of the County's Assistant Groundsman for many years and a popular figure at the County Ground; now, in retirement, he continues to help the Club part-time.

(b)

(b) Grace Fuller joined Brigadier Green in 1946 as his sole secretarial assistant. Mrs Fuller is still with the Club today and her knowledge of the Club's finances and, in particular, its membership is extremely valuable. In 1976 a presentation was made to her to mark 30 years faithful service to the Club. Mrs. Lorna Brierley is seated at the desk.

(c)

(c) Richard Stevens is the present Head Groundsman. He too has won the County Groundsman of the Year award, in 1978 his second season with the County.

Club and a corner-stone of its administration today.

Paul Foley and Henry Foster set the Club along the pathway in first-class cricket and their foresight, ambition, and example has been abundantly justified. As a result of the steps they were courageous enough to take much pleasure and fulfilment has been provided for the players, members and supporters of Worcestershire County Cricket Club.

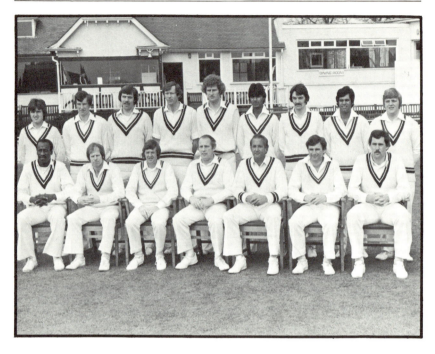

Worcestershire XI 1979: Standing (L to R): B.J.R. Jones, C.N. Boyns, G.G. Watson, J. Cumbes, A.P. Pridgeon, D.N. Patel, P.A. Neale, Younis Ahmed, D.J. Humphries

Seated: V.A. Holder, E.J.O. Hemsley, G.M. Turner, N. Gifford (Captain), B.L. D'Oliveira, J.A. Ormrod, J.D. Inchmore.

Along the way men such as Maurice Jewell, the Foster and Cobham families, Cyril Smith, Gilbert Ashton, Fred Root, Doc Gibbons, Reg Perks, Brig. Mike Green, Dick Howorth, Roly Jenkins, Don Kenyon, Sir George Dowty, Joe Lister, Tom Graveney, Roy Booth and Norman Gifford and many, many others besides have taken up their example and their ambition.

Worcestershire County Cricket Club is the smallest of the first-class Counties. It survives, and thrives, as a Champion County. It *may* face some dark days in the future; there *will* be many more good days, more good cricket and, it is to be hoped, cricket that is fun and which truly serves the interests of the game and the "much required Worcestershire County Cricket Club".

WORCESTERSHIRE C.C.C. – A CHRONOLOGY

YEAR	CAPTAIN	POSITION IN CHAMP.^P	LEADING* BATSMAN AND BOWLER
1844			Played Shrops. at Hartlebury; return match at Shrewsbury. Both games lost.
1847			Worcester County C.C. had 58 members. Played against City of Worcester. Matches played at Ombersley.
1848			XXII of Worcester played All-England XI at Powick Ham. Lost by 123 runs. W.G. Grace born.
1851			XXII of Worcester lost to All-England XI by 23 runs. Match played on ground at rear of Talbot Inn, Barbourne. First appearance of a member of Lyttelton family for Worcs.
1855			Amalgamation of City and County cricket clubs. Pitchcroft used for home games.
1856			Matches played at St. John's.
1859			Pleasure Gardens in the Arboretum used for home games.

111

YEAR	CAPTAIN	POSITION IN CHAMP.P	LEADING* BATSMAN AND BOWLER	
1865				Official founding of W.C.C.C. Boughton Park used for home matches until c. 1898.
1895	H.K. Foster			Paul Foley and H.K. Foster instrumental in founding Minor Counties Championship. W.C.C.C. tied with Norfolk and Durham for title.
1896	H.K. Foster		H.K. Foster E.G. Arnold	First in Minor Counties Championship. New Road ground rented from Dean and Chapter, Worcester Cathedral.
1897	H.K. Foster		E.G. Arnold E. Bramley-Martin	Minor Counties' Champions
1898	H.K. Foster		R.E. Foster G.A. Wilson	Minor Counties' Champions
1899	H.K. Foster	12th	W.L. Foster R.D. Burrows	Entered First-class County Championship. T. Straw dismissed "obstructing the field".
1900	R.E. Foster	12th	R.E. Foster C. Bannister	H.K. Foster first to score 1000 runs for County; G.A. Wilson took 100 wickets for County.

Year	Captain	Position	Professionals	Notes
1901	H.K. Foster	11th	R.E. Foster A. Bird	S. Africans visited Worcester (match tied).
1902	H.K. Foster	9th	R.E. Foster A. Bird	E.G. Arnold did the Double. Australians visited Worcester.
1903	H.K. Foster	6th	H.K. Foster E.G. Arnold	Arnold achieved Double. W.C.C.C. dismissed for 24 by Yorkshire – match ended in day. R.E. Foster 287 v. Australia.
1904	H.K. Foster	13th	F.L. Bowley E.G. Arnold	Arnold achieved Double.
1905	H.K. Foster	8th	R.E. Foster G.A. Wilson	Batting good with seven innings over 300 runs, including three over 400, one over 500, one over 600. Arnold's fourth Double. Northants joined County Championship. County played at Stourbridge.
1906	H.K. Foster	14th	E.G. Arnold A. Bird	Arnold scored six centuries. County achieved highest score 633 (v. Warks) and Leics. (701–4) recorded highes score against County.
1907	H.K. Foster	2nd	G.N. Foster J.A. Cuffe	Runners-up in Championship. H.K., R.E. and G.N. Foster all averaged 40. Second XI run for only time prior to 1948

YEAR	CAPTAIN	POSITION IN CHAMP.P	LEADING* BATSMAN AND BOWLER	
1908	H.K. Foster	6th	H.K. Foster G.H. Simpson-Hayward	Five Fosters appeared in team. Hon. C. Lyttelton (Camb. Univ.) played.
1909	H.K. Foster	9th	E.G. Arnold G.H. Simpson-Hayward	Arnold 200* and 10-114 in match v. Warwicks, and with Burns established present record for 5th wicket partnership.
1910	H.K. Foster	13th	H.K. Foster G.H. Simpson-Hayward	Bale's wicket-keeping regarded second only to Strudwick. County played at Dudley.
1911	G.K. Simpson-Hayward	9th	H.K. Foster R.D. Burrows	Cuffe achieved Double. 12 matches won but gates poor and doubts existed about continuing in 1912. Grand Bazaar saved situation. Burrows achieved record for distance travelled by bail. County played home match at Bourneville.
1912	G.H. Simpson-Hayward	16th	F.L. Bowley G.H. Simpson-Hayward	Bottom of table. Practically no appearances by Fosters.
1913	H.K. Foster	12th	G.N. Foster R.D. Burrows	F. Chester (17 years) scored 3 centuries and took 43 wickets. Financial position very serious; only efforts of Lord Cobham, Lord Dudley,

				Lord Plymouth and Judge Amphlett enabled Club to keep going.
1914	Lt. Col. W.H. Taylor	14th	F.L. Bowley J.A. Cuffe	F. Bowley scored 276 v. Hants at Dudley – highest individul score for County.
1919	Lt. Col. W.H. Taylor			Worcestershire did not re-enter Championship.
1920	Maj. M.F.S. Jewell	15th	F.L. Bowley C.A. Preece	Poor season after Championship programme resumed.
1921	Maj. M.F.S. Jewell	14th	F.A. Pearson H.A. Gilbert	G. Ashton captained Cambridge University and played for A.C. MacLaren's England XI which beat the Australians. Glamorgan entered County Championship. County played at Kidderminster.
1922	Lt. Col. W.H. Taylor	17th	H.L. Higgins F.A. Pearson	F.L. Bowley retired G. Ashton debut for County.
1923	M.K. Foster	15th	M.K. Foster C.F. Root	C.F. Root introduced his "leg theory" bowling. F.A. Pearson achieved Double at age of 42.
1924	M.K. Foster	14th	M.K. Foster C.F. Root	L.G Crawley and W.V. Fox banned from playing for County ("not properly qualified") having played for two seasons.

YEAR	CAPTAIN	POSITION IN CHAMP.P	LEADING* BATSMAN AND BOWLER	
1925	M.K. Foster	16th	M.K. Foster C.F. Root	F. Root 219 wickets. 37 players appeared for County.
1926	Maj. M.F.S. Jewell	17th	M.K. Foster C.F. Root	Eight professionals on staff. F.A. Pearson, aged 46, retired at end of season.
1927	C.B. Ponsonby	17th	L.R. Serrurier C.F. Root	County bowled out for less than 100 on 13 occasions. H.H.I. Gibbons made debut.
1928	Maj. M.F.S. Jewell	17th	J.B. Higgins C.F. Root	Five players scored 1000 runs, F. Root completed Double and yet County failed to win one match. M. Nichol scored century on debut. C.F. Walters and R.T.D. Perks joined the County and started qualification period.
1929	Maj. M.F.S. Jewell and Hon. J.B. Coventry	16th	H.H.I. Gibbons C.F. Root	Poor season; on three occasions totals of 500 runs were hit against the County.
1930	Hon. J.B. Coventry	10th	M. Nichol G.W. Brook	R.T.D. Perks' Championship debut. D. Bradman scored 235 on first visit to Worcester.
1931	C.F. Walters	14th	M. Nichol C.F. Root	F. Root took 123 wickets at under 16 runs each.

Year	Captain	Pos	Batsmen/Bowlers	Notes
1932	C.F. Walters	17th	C.F. Walters L. Wright	F. Root retired. Nichol frequently absent through illness.
1933	C.F. Walters	15th	C.F. Walters P.F. Jackson	Gibbons, Walters and Nichol each scored 2000 runs; Walters established W.C.C.C. record of 7 centuries in season. 26 century partnerships achieved by County.
1934	C.F. Walters	16th	C.F. Walters R.T.D. Perks	Gibbons scored 2654 – highest aggregate in season for County. M. Nichol died tragically at Chelmsford. Bradman scored 206 on second visit with Australians. County reported to have made profit for first time in its first-class history.
1935	C.F. Walters	12th	C.F. Walters R. Howorth	Nine Championship wins. Howorth (123 wickets) showed great improvement. The horse (aged 34) which pulled the roller died. New LBW Law introduced.
1936	Hon. C.J. Lyttelton	12th	H.H.I. Gibbons R. Howorth	Famous victory against Yorkshire at Stourbridge. Nursery formed (of young players) and friendly games arranged with neighbouring Second XIs. S. Buller qualified and took over wicket-keeping from B.W. Quaife.

YEAR	CAPTAIN	POSITION IN CHAMP.P	LEADING* BATSMAN AND BOWLER	
1937	Hon. C.J. Lyttelton	15th	H.H.I. Gibbons S.H. Martin	17 matches lost. Four bowlers (Perks, Howorth, Martin and Jackson) took 100 wickets. Martin did the Double.
1938	Hon. C.J. Lyttelton	11th	H.H.I. Gibbons R.J. Crisp	Bradman scored 258 on third visit to Worcester. Gibbons averaged 44 runs in 53 innings in Benefit Year. C.H. Palmer and R.O. Jenkins made debut.
1939	Hon. C.J. Lyttelton	7th	A.P. Singleton R.T.D. Perks	R.T.D. Perks visited S. Africa with MCC and played in 5th Test which after 10 days was left drawn. Howorth and Martin achieved Double. C. Bull killed in car accident in which S. Buller also injured. Eleven wins and one match tied.
1940–45				R.E.S. Wyatt and A.F. "Spinney" Lane arranged occasional matches. Lane, G.W. Nicholls and C.G.D. Smith kept Club alive during War.
1946	A.P. Singleton	10th	R.E.S. Wyatt P.F. Jackson	Howorth only English player to achieve Double. R.E.S. Wyatt and A.F.T. White joined County.

1947	**A.F.T. White**	7th	**C.H. Palmer** **R. Howorth**	Highest recorded flood at Worcester. Howorth 1500 runs and 150 wickets; also took a wicket with first ball in Test Match (v. S. Africa at Oval). Yarnold leading 'keeper in country. Perks' Benefit £2950 – then a Worcs. record. County subscription £2.2.0 (£2.10p).
1948	**A.F.T. White**	10th	**M.L.Y. Ainsworth** **R. Howorth**	Bradman's fourth visit to Worcester, scored 107. Second XI established.
1949	**A.F.T White** and **R.E.S. Wyatt**	3rd	**E. Cooper** **R. Howorth**	Jubilee in first-class cricket. Twelve wins. Kenyon, Cooper, Outschoorn and Bird scored 1000 runs. Howorth and Perks took 100 wickets. Jenkins did the Double including hat-trick in each innings v. Surrey. Yarnold captured 110 victims. Outschoorn took 55 catches. J.D. Robertson (Middlesex) scored 331* against County in a day.
1950	**R.E.S. Wyatt**	6th	**D. Kenyon** **G.H. Chesterton**	H.K. Foster died. Kenyon scored 2000 runs.
1951	**R.E.S. Wyatt**	4th	**D. Kenyon** **R. Howorth**	Kenyon 2000 runs. Yarnold captured 7 (including 6 stumped) v. Scotland. 27

119

YEAR	CAPTAIN	POSITION IN CHAMP.P	LEADING* BATSMAN AND BOWLER	
				century partnerships for County. Jackson and Howorth retired, each after taking 1000 wickets for County. Supporters' Association formed on 14th June.
1952	R.E. Bird	14th	D. Kenyon K. Lobban	Kenyon 2439 runs; Jenkins achieved Double.
1953	R.E. Bird	15th	D. Kenyon R.O. Jenkins	Kenyon and Richardson scored over 2000 in season. Kenyon hit first century by Worcs. player v. Australia. Perks took 2000th wicket and Jenkins his 1000th wicket.
1954	R.E. Bird	11th	D. Kenyon G.H. Chesterton	Kenyon 2500 runs (and first to 1000 runs). J. Lister appointed Assistant Secretary. New Score Board unveiled. C.F. Root died.
1955	R.T.D. Perks	15th	P.E. Richardson G.H. Chesterton	R.T.D. Perks appointed first professional Captain; retired at end of season after taking 100 wickets (for 16th time) and 2233 wickets in all. Testimonial £2600. Yarnold retired. Kenyon scored 2000 runs for sixth time. M. Horton achieved Double in first full season. Ground flooded in June.

1956	**P.E. Richardson**	9th	**D. Kenyon** **R.O. Jenkins**	One of wettest summers ever. R. Booth succeeded H. Yarnold.
1957	**P.E. Richardson**	16th	**D. Kenyon** **K.J. Aldridge**	Flavell 100 wickets for first time. Kenyon scored 2000 runs and became heaviest scorer for the County (23,067 runs). P.E. and D.W. Richardson played in Test Match v. W. Indies. Queen Elizabeth II visited County Ground.
1958	**P.E. Richardson**	9th	**P.E. Richardson** **K.J. Aldridge**	R.O. Jenkins retired. N. Gifford joined staff.
1959	**D. Kenyon**	14th	**M.J. Horton** **L. Coldwell**	Seven batsmen scored 1000 runs. 25 century partnerships. Booth scored 1042 runs and captured 89 wickets.
1960	**D. Kenyon**	13th	**G. Dews** **N. Gifford**	R. Booth 101 victims behind stumps. Gifford headed averages in debut season. Subscriptions increased to £3.3.0 (£3.15p).
1961	**D. Kenyon**	4th	**R.G.A. Headley** **J.A. Flavell**	Sixteen Championship Matches won. Four bowlers: Flavell, Coldwell, Gifford, Horton, took 100 wickets. Horton did the Double. D.W. Richardson's County record of 65 catches in season. T.W. Graveney joined

YEAR	CAPTAIN	POSITION IN CHAMP.P	LEADING* BATSMAN AND BOWLER	
				staff but unable to play Championship cricket until 12 months' qualification completed. G. Dews retired after scoring 16,856 runs and taking 346 catches (County record).
1962	D. Kenyon	2nd	T.W. Graveney L. Coldwell	Kenyon and Graveney passed 30,000 runs aggregate for careers. Second XI won Second Eleven Championship.
1963	D. Kenyon	15th	T.W. Graveney N. Gifford	Gillette Cup introduced. County in first-ever Final (v. Sussex) and Gifford was Man of Match. Second XI retained title. Distinction between amateurs and professionals abolished in cricket.
1964	D. Kenyon	1st	T.W. Graveney J.A. Standen	County Champions. Booth 100 wickets and became leading wicket-keeper for Worcestershire. B.L. D'Oliveira qualified for County.
1965	D. Kenyon	1st	T.W. Graveney J.A. Flavell	Championship retained. County made World tour. Centenary Year.
1966	D. Kenyon	2nd	T.W. Graveney	Gillette Cup Finalists.

			J.A. Flavell	D'Oliveira played for England. Ormrod 1000 runs for first time. M. Horton retired.
1967	D. Kenyon	5th	T.W. Graveney J.A. Flavell	Kenyon retired after scoring 37,000 runs in career; took first and last wicket in first-class cricket. Flavell retired after taking 1507 wickets for Worcestershire.
1968	T.W. Graveney	7th	T.W. Graveney B.L. D'Oliveira	T.W. Graveney awarded OBE. G.M. Turner 1000 runs for first time. D'Oliveira selected for England's tour of S. Africa which was cancelled by S. African government. Booth retired; his career bag of 1021 victims is the best for a Worcestershire 'keeper, and he also took 101 for Yorkshire before joining the County.
1969	T.W. Graveney	12th	E.J.O. Hemsley D.N.F. Slade	Coldwell retired; his 1076 wickets were obtained more cheaply than any other Worcs. bowler who has taken 1000 wickets. Turner carried bat for New Zealand against England at Lord's. D'Oliveira awarded OBE. John Player League introduced. Ground flooded in June.
1970	T.W. Graveney	6th	T.W. Graveney N. Gifford	Graveney retired at end of season. Turner scored 10

YEAR	CAPTAIN	POSITION IN CHAMP.P	LEADING* BATSMAN AND BOWLER	
				centuries in season (and was once run out for 99) – a Worcs. record.
1971	N. Gifford	15th	R.G.A. Headley B.L. D'Oliveira	John Player League Champions. J. Lister resigns to become Secretary of Yorkshire C.C.C. Subscriptions increased to £5.00.
1972	N. Gifford	7th	G.M. Turner N. Gifford	Benson and Hedges Cup introduced; County Championship reduced to 20 matches. Worcs. semi-finalists in Gillette Cup.
1973	N. Gifford	6th	R.G.A. Headley V.A. Holder	Benson & Hedges Cup Finalists (v. Kent) and Gillette Cup Semi-finalists. Turner scores 1000 runs by end of May, for New Zealand.
1974	N. Gifford	1st	G.M. Turner V.A. Holder	County Champions and Gillette Cup Semi-Finalists. County stages Test Trial. New Road stand has canopy built over it. N. Gifford's benefit £11,047, a Worcs. record.
1975	N. Gifford	10th	Imran Khan B.L. D'Oliveira	County runners-up in John Player League. First Prudential World Cup, staged in U.K. D'Oliveira's Benefit £27,000.

124

Year	Captain	Position	Top Players	Notes
1976	**N. Gifford**	11th	**G.M. Turner** **Imran Khan**	Benson and Hedges Cup Finalists (v. Kent). Patel (17 yrs) scores maiden century. Turner scores 1000 runs in the season in over-limit cricket. County Committee reduced in size and restructured.
1977	**N. Gifford**	13th	**B.L. D'Oliveira** **J.D. Inchmore**	County Ground purchased from Dean and Chapter of Catherdral. Imran Khan departs to Sussex. Lord Cobham and Reg Perks die. Subscriptions increased to £10.00
1978	**N. Gifford**	15th	**G.M. Turner** **B.L. D'Oliveira**	Fourth in John Player League. P Neale scores 1000 runs for first time. N. Gifford awarded MBE. C.H. Palmer elected President MCC. Death of Major M.F.S Jewell.
1979	**N. Gifford**	2nd	**Younis Ahmed** **N. Gifford**	Third in John Player League (Turner becomes leading run scorer in this competition) and Quarter-Finalists in Benson & Hedges Cup. County stages I.C.C. Trophy ('mini' World Cup) Final. Prudential World Cup staged in U.K. Subscription £13.00

* These rankings are based on the averages taken from the County Year Book – or Wisden where no Year Book is available – for batsmen playing ten or more innings and for bowlers bowling at least 100 overs and taking 10 wickets).

Captains Gallery

H.K. Foster captained Worcestershire in its Minor County days and led the County to four Minor Counties' Championships from 1895–1898. Henry Foster was Captain in 1899 when Worcestershire became a first-class County, but handed over the reins to his brother, R.E., in the following season. He resumed the captaincy in 1901 and continued for 10 seasons. He is thus the longest-serving Captain of the County. During his captaincy the County were runners-up in the County Championship in 1907.

R.E. Foster Possibly the most gifted of the Foster brothers, Reginald Foster led the County for one season only, at the age of 22, in the same season in which he also captained Oxford University. He played much less for the County than his elder brother but doubtless his health (he was a diabetic) was the prime reason for this. However, he was also to play for England whom he captained in three Tests.

G.H.T. Simpson-Hayward captained Worcestershire in 1911 and 1912. He was a true amateur who once declined to play for the Gentlemen v. Players as he wished to go to Austria to see a rare flower which bloomed only briefly at the time of the match. It was in his second term of captaincy that the County was placed bottom of the Championship for the first time.

Lt. Col W.H. Taylor Captain in 1914 and again in 1922, is remembered by those who played under him as a warm-hearted man with an irrespressible sense of fun and a keen desire for the game to be played brightly. He was a

useful fast medium bowler with a lithe action. He played an immense but unobstrusive part in keeping the County flag flying in the years either side of the First World War. M.F.S. Jewell was his brother-in-law.

Maj. M.F.S. Jewell His role in the history of Worcestershire C.C.C. is of the greatest importance. During his three spells of captaincy (1920-21, 1926 and 1928-29) the County's fortunes were at their lowest both in financial terms and in playing strength and results. His stout-hearted determination to revive the County's health was boundless and the complete dedication with which he set about improving the County's finances brought its due rewards. Without him Worcestershire may not have long survived as a first-class County.

Maurice Foster was a very good player who, had he played in a stronger side, almost certainly would have emulated the more fruitful achievements of his older brothers. During his captaincy, from 1923-1925, he managed to keep the County off the bottom of the table which was a feat in itself when it is remembered that the professional staff was very small and the County had to rely on a large number of amateurs. Some, like Foster himself, Ashton and Maclean, were gifted but not regularly available; others were more often available but not so well blessed with talent. Foster's own performances and his lead were most important.

Cecil Brabazon Ponsonby was the first, and to date, the last, wicket-keeper officially to be appointed County Captain. He played for the County between 1911 and 1928 and was Captain in 1927. In thirteen seasons he played in only

74 matches, and captured 82 victims (71 ct. 11 st.). His 127 innings averaged under 8 runs each.

126

Hon. J.B. Coventry appeared for the County between 1920 and 1935. He took over the captaincy from Maurice Jewell midway through 1929 and was re-appointed Captain for the following season although he was able to play only occasionally. In that second season however the County rose to tenth place in the Championship. John Coventry was a right hand bat and slow left arm bowler. In his 75 appearances for the County he averaged just under 15 runs per innings and his 16 wickets cost 45 runs each.

C.F. Walters joined Worcestershire from Glamorgan in 1928 and had to spend two years qualifying for his new County. He was appointed Captain at the age of 24 and was to lead the County for five seasons until 1935. Cyril Walters had shown much promise when with Glamorgan; now for Worcestershire his batting blossomed and was likened to that of the greats of cricket's Golden Age. Later (in 1933 and 1934) he was to play for England on 11 occasions and, as a result of R.E.S. Wyatt's illness, captained England in his first Test v. Australia.

Hon. C.J. Lyttelton succeeded Cyril Walters and captained the County until the outbreak of the Second World War. He was an inspired and inspiring leader much loved by his players to whom he was "Skip". Under his command Worcestershire rose to 7th in the Championship table. The Cobham family has been as closely involved with Worcestershire as has its other notable family, the Fosters, and Charles Lyttelton greatly enjoyed his own association with the County.

On assuming his father's title as Lord Cobham he was to become heavily involved in state and public duties, but throughout this time his interest in Worcestershire C.C.C. remained undiminished. In 1977, to mutual delight, he was elected President of the Club but, sadly, died shortly after taking office.

A.P. Singleton Sandy Singleton appeared occasionally for the County before the War (from 1934) in his vacations from Oxford University. When the War ended cricket gained a great following from a public eager for a return to normality. That same feeling was generated amongst county cricketers, but even allowing for that ambient atmosphere Sandy Singleton's captaincy was just what was needed. He gave a splendid, adventurous lead as Captain and his all-

round example was excellent. As Captain he was greatly admired by his players.

A.F.T. White led the side in 1947 and 1948 and then shared the captaincy with R.E.S. Wyatt in the following summer. A jovial and good humoured man, Alan White allowed his sense of fun to rub off on to his team who responded to his adventurous and attacking cricket. When his playing days were over he continued to serve the County as a member of the Club's General Committee.

R.E.S. Wyatt joined Worcestershire in 1946. By then, aged 45, he had played for Warwickshire for many seasons and had appeared in 40 Tests for England, captaining his country in 15 of those matches. In 1949, when he shared the captaincy with Alan White, the County rose to 3rd place in the Championship. In the two succeeding seasons Bob Wyatt was in sole charge and the County retained its new found form and success. His experience was of great benefit to the team, to individual players, and not least himself. At 50, what he lacked in youthful athleticism was more than compensated for by his greater experience and he continued to get his share of runs and wickets, even, on occasions, opening the bowling with Reg Perks.

R.E. Bird captained the team from 1952 to 1954 during a period of transition when many of the pre-war stalwarts were coming to the end of their careers and younger players were beginning the process of establishing themselves in the County XI. Ronnie Bird was a right hand bat and medium-paced bowler. His batting was sound and determined and it regularly received the praises of the Tourists, against whom he invariably seemed to play well.

R.T.D. Perks had been a member of the County staff for twenty-eight years by 1955 when he was appointed County Captain, the first professional elected to that office. Reg Perks was a universally popular cricketer who proved to be a sound Captain. Whilst his service and loyalty to Worcestershire may be equalled it will never be exceeded.

P.E. Richardson was the man chosen to succed Reg Perks. Peter Richardson was an amateur batsman who performed admirably for Worcestershire and for England. In his first season as Captain his enthusiasm for the game was imparted to the rest of the team, but in his second season it was felt that the responsibilities he carried (for County and country) affected his captaincy. In 1958 the County recovered to 9th place and Peter seemed to have regained his zest for the job. Subsequently he moved to Kent and played for that County.

Don Kenyon was asked to lead the side in 1959 when Richardson transferred his allegiance to Kent. His first two seasons did not bring any great improvement in Worcestershire's fortunes but then came the leap forward. From that time, and with the exception of one season, Kenyon kept his team in the top five places of the County table. For two of those seasons Worcestershire won the County Championship and also reached the Gillette Cup Final on two occasions. A truly Champion Captain and, to quote Rev. Chignell's dedication to Kenyon in his second volume on Worcestershire, "a Champion of Leaders and a Leader of Champions".

Tom Graveney, one of cricket's great players, took over the captaincy from Worcestershire's most successful skipper. If any-one had the right background for the task it was Tom Graveney, an exquisitely gifted batsman and the most experienced player of the day. Despite another transitional period resulting from the retirement of senior members of Kenyon's Championship team, Graveney kept the County's fortunes steady and, more importantly, set them forward to a new Championship era.

Norman Gifford is Worcestershire's second Champion Captain as under his captaincy in 1974, Worcestershire won the County Championship for the third time. Three years earlier, in his first season as skipper, 1971, he had led the County to the John Player League title. Add to this the team's appearances in the Benson and Hedges Cup Finals in 1973 and 1976 and it can be seen that Norman Gifford, who joined the County at the start of Kenyon's reign as Captain, had learnt much from a Champion Captain and richly deserves to share that same title and recognition.

128